SOLOMON AND SHEBA

# solomon

AND

# sheba

JAY WILLIAMS

RANDOM HOUSE, NEW YORK

*This book is dedicated to the memory of
my grandparents*

Biblical quotations in the text are taken from *The Bible, An American
Translation*, edited by J. M. Powis Smith and Edgar J. Goodspeed. The
University of Chicago Press.

# PART ONE

# 1
## THE LION

The two young men checked their horses on the hill crest and sat looking out over the plain. The early sun over their shoulders threw their long shadows down before them, over the gray shale almost to the grasslands below. Behind them, their hunting party—all on horseback or on mules—stopped, and the young villager who acted as their guide set his arm over his eyes and looked up at them, squinting with a smile. The sun's rays aureoled them, gleaming upon their hair and beards, and he thought to himself how comely they appeared, clearly not as other men, but princes upon whom Yahweh had placed his seal. The taller of the two, Adonijah, had a leonine air, his tawny hair hanging like a mane to his broad shoulders, his eyes clear and cold with yellowish lights in them. But it was upon the other, the younger, that the gaze of the villager rested longest.

It was so with all men, for having looked once upon Solomon the son of David, they must look again. There was about the youth a certain grace and sweetness, like that of his mother Bathsheba when she was young, when, of all the king's wives, she had been his best beloved. Dignity, too, sat upon his tall and slender frame, lithe as a dancer's and yet well-muscled and hardy. From his mother came the thin, curved nose, the olive skin, the dark brown of his hair and soft beard, but the large lustrous eyes were those of his father, eyes that drew after him all who looked in them.

The villager said, "My lords, the track leads down on the south-ward side. In the plain below, you may dismount and hunt."

Adonijah, resting his hands upon his corded thighs, turned to Solomon. "Well, then, shall we descend? Or does my brother wish to cast about here in the hills for such game as we may find?"

"No," said Solomon, "let us go down. But do not bring the nets, for I have seen a gazelle struggling with broken legs in the meshes before this. Surely, we need not torture beasts for our meat?"

Adonijah's laugh echoed among the rocks. "My brother has the heart of a girl, weeping for her one lamb. Nevertheless, be it as you say. There will be more sport."

He shook the reins. The villager trotted ahead, sure-footed as a goat on the narrow track. The party rode after, in single file, the dust rising about them.

In the shadow of the hills they dismounted and left the horses and pack mules to the servants. Beaters, brought from the village of En Rimmon, went out into the grass on either side, carrying sticks. The main party spread in a long line, some thirty men with Solomon and Adonijah, each followed by his armor-bearer, near one end where the game would soonest leap forth. Solomon bore two javelins, for few could equal him at spear-casting, but Adonijah carried his great bow of wood backed with sinew, with which he could send an arrow through the triple thickness of a bull's-hide shield.

Uttering shrill cries, the beaters moved off. Soon after, the company also began walking, the grass rustling against their legs. As they went, they spread further apart so that no man might be struck by a stray arrow. The sun was higher and the air warm and limpid, as yet unhazed by heat.

Solomon walked as if alone, feeling the sun between his shoulder blades, delighting in the morning. On his left hand the gray-blue hills fell away; only now and again a great rock or heap of rocks emerged on the plain, like an upthrust root of the heights. Walking so, he could forget all things, even the hunt, in the pleasure he took in the land. His gaze passed with affection over the rippling prairie, the spiny trunks and small leaves of an acacia grove, a bird that flew, calling, far above, and the dark figures of his friends moving knee-high through the bending grass in a long irregular crescent out upon his right.

He turned to his armor-bearer and saw that the young man trudged slowly, with his eyes on the ground. He was two or three years younger than the prince; his name was Zabud the son of Nathan, a Bethlehemite.

"It is a fair morning," Solomon said.

"As my lord wishes," replied the lad without enthusiasm.

"Why, then, do you walk with eyes cast down as if searching for a lost coin?"

Zabud smiled faintly. "No, my lord, I search for my lost breakfast.

Last night, when we lay in En Rimmon, I ate too much of the roast meat and all night I rolled in torment. This morning I could not keep food down, and my head aches."

"Was it the meat? Or was it that the son of Nathan drank too freely of the southern wine?"

"It may have been so," said Zabud, reddening.

"You are not yet of an age to carouse with old men," laughed Solomon. "Sit down in the shade of this tree and rest. Later we shall find you another breakfast."

"My lord is kind," Zabud sighed. He lowered himself to the ground under an acacia. "In truth, it is as if a sword were thrust behind my eyeballs."

Leaving him there, Solomon went on. But now his tranquillity was disturbed; that chance phrase, "a sword thrust behind my eyeballs," had awakened in him an ugly memory, the recollection of that day at Baal-hazor, the day of the sheep-shearing.

He had been only a boy, then, and yet the memory of the day was imprinted clearly on his mind in every ugly detail.

They had all gone up together to his brother Absalom's house at Baal-hazor for the festival. All the sons of the king were thus gathered together: Amnon, the eldest, the son of Ahinoam the Jezreelitess; Chileab the son of Abigail; Absalom the son of Maacah, handsomest of all the princes and dearest to King David's heart; Adonijah the son of Haggith, already tall and powerful beyond his years; Shephetiah the son of Abital; Ithream the son of Eglah; and Solomon, the last-born. He remembered the taste of honey-cakes, the sweetmeats of crushed sesame seed, the fresh warm milk. He remembered how they had all come to the long table together, in the shade, and how they had eaten and drunk and their tongues had been loosened by wine. There had been singing and laughter, and the smell of the wool and the distant bleating of sheep.

He had been sitting beside Amnon, and his brother had said to him, "Drink, now, little one. For wine is warming; even for children wine may bring merriment."

Absalom, sitting at the foot of the table, had leaned forward on one elbow, saying, "And for women also. Was it with wine, Amnon, that you plied my sister Tamar?"

A hush had fallen over the table. Solomon, looking at the eldest brother, had seen his face grow white as curds. But he said nothing.

And again Absalom said, "Tell me, brother, was it with wine that you made my sister Tamar drunken, so that you might lie with her in our father's house? Or was it with wine that you first bolstered up your own spirit, to do such a thing? Was it wine that gave you courage to cast her out, when you had violated her, saying to your servant, 'Put this woman from my presence, and bolt the door after her'?"

Absalom's face, so smooth and serene, had been flushed with anger and hatred; the words were spat out of him in jerks. Amnon, before his brother's wrath, could only sit staring, wide-eyed, like a sheep. All at once, Absalom had sprung to his feet, overturning his wine cup, and in a voice hoarse and terrible with passion, cried, "Strike down Amnon!"

With that, two serving men had sprung forward, one on either side of Amnon. Before he could move, one of them had struck him with a dagger. He had stabbed for the throat but missed his aim, and the weapon went into Amnon's skull at the temple and there stuck fast. The second man had caught him by the throat, as a slaughterer catches a lamb, and stabbed him in the breast and again in the side. Blood spattered the white tablecloth and warm drops fell on Solomon's arm.

So that day had ended in murder, that began with rejoicing, and so it was with Israel that brother slew brother and kinsman fought with kinsman; and soon after, Absalom had revolted against his father and had himself been killed.

Deep sorrow welled up in Solomon. Not only for his brothers but for the blood that had been too long shed in the land. The desire for the crown brought war and death with it, and had not the House of Kish, the sons of King Saul, been utterly exterminated? Even in himself, Solomon felt the stirring of this desire; he sometimes said to himself, "When I am king . . ." altering it swiftly to, "When my brother is king, for surely as he is the elder our father's choice will fall upon him." But still he could not altogether put down his imagination, and his wish for peace was so strong that he would think, If it should be the will of Yahweh that I might ever be crowned with the crown of Israel and Judah, then I will establish a rule of love, and peace, and order such as has never been known . . .

A movement, half-seen from the corner of his eye, brought him from his musings. He had wandered, unthinking, closer to the hills, and he stood beside a jutting ledge where tumbled boulders were heaped up and had rolled into the plain, as if idly tossed by the hand of one of the giants of ancient days. Low, thorny shrubs grew thickly about them. A rank odor came to him, a sweetish feral smell. At the same time, what he had taken to be a heap of yellowish clay stirred, rose up, and was revealed to be a young lion.

For a long moment, they regarded each other. Solomon felt no fear whatever. He had only once before seen a lion so close, and that was at the court of his father's friend, Hiram of Tyre, where the king, whose curiosity about the earth's creatures was lively and profound, kept many beasts of different sorts in enclosures in a great park. But the lions there had been torpid with captivity, dull-eyed and spiritless. This one was younger, sleeker despite the dust on his coat, alert and curious. His round eyes watched Solomon with unwinking objectivity, with the calmness of one who knows his power.

All the joy of the morning had returned to Solomon with the sight of this beautiful and regal creature. Mystical exaltation filled him; the words of a song of David entered his mind unbidden, and he smiled to think of it:

> Great are the works of the Lord,
> To be studied by all who delight in them.
> Majestic and glorious is his work,
> And his righteousness endures forever.

Like the clang of a chord on the phrase, there came a loud shout. The lion raised his head and took a step. Solomon turned his head also. It was Adonijah who had called a warning. He stood nearly two hundred paces off, and although it was an impossible range, he raised his bow; he drew the string to his ear, and shot. The black shaft arched high and rushed down. Nearly spent, it yet had force enough to penetrate the lion's flank.

The beast roared. And Solomon came to himself, realizing his danger. Before it could charge, he had hurled the first of his javelins. The range was short; the spear stood quivering in the lion's throat. Solomon had dropped down on one knee, holding the second javelin braced against the ground to receive the animal's rush, but there was no need. The lion coughed black blood, and slowly sank down, breaking the spear-shaft with its weight.

Even as he shot, Adonijah had bounded forward, and now from closer in sent another arrow into the beast.

"He is dead," said Solomon.

"Is my brother unhurt?" Adonijah's face was flushed with running.

Solomon stood and placed a hand on Adonijah's arm. "I am untouched, thanks to my brother's warning."

He had no wish to stint his gratitude, and yet . . . and yet, he thought, surely the lion would not have charged. Surely he would have given way before me. We would have gone our separate ways, for there was no enmity between us. But this could not be spoken.

"My brother is a mighty archer," he said, smiling. "No other in the land of Israel could have sped such a shot."

Adonijah's teeth shone in his beard. "It was but a little way, and a little way further, as the song of the maiden says." He walked to the side of the lion and pushed at it with his toe. "This is a fine pelt," he said. "I will have Jehiel take it off for you, for he is a master of the skinning knife."

Solomon looked down at the lion also, sighing. "Let my brother keep this skin," he said, "as a small part of my thanks."

"It is a good gift. I will take it."

The others came panting up, among them Zabud, pale and stricken to think he had left his lord to face danger alone, but he had fallen asleep under the acacia and it was only the roar of the lion that had awakened him.

"I am a fool," he lamented. "Worthless—good for nothing—"

"That is the truth," said a tall, dark-skinned Ephraimite named Nebat. He was a foppish young man whose father had left him a large estate; he was a close friend of Adonijah's. "This dead dog should be cast out," he said contemptuously. "Worthless, indeed, to desert the son of Bathsheba. How can he be trusted in war?"

"No," said Solomon, "Zabud did not desert me. I commanded him to remain behind."

"Nevertheless, he should be punished. An armor-bearer's place is beside his lord, whatever the command," said another man. He was a captain over a hundred, and his name was Joel the son of Abner; he had the reputation of being a fierce warrior.

"Surely the son of Abner cannot believe that," said Solomon, smiling at his armor-bearer. Zabud looked at him with mournful eyes, scarcely daring to return the smile. "The servant must do his master's bidding though it tear his heart to do so. If it were otherwise, the servant would rule over the prince. No, no, let him be. In any case, the lion is dead."

Jehiel, the armor-bearer of Adonijah, was already at work with his knife, slitting the skin of the lion's belly. He looked up and said, "It was a great deed. See, my lords, the javelin has gone in for half its length, and severed the great blood vessel of the neck. But my lord Adonijah's arrow struck a hand's breadth in the flank even though it was shot from two hundred paces. There is much here to boast of."

"A brother helped by a brother is like a fortified city," said Solomon. "Come, friends, let us continue the hunt."

"May we find gazelles, now," said a moon-faced, cheerful youth.

"Others may eat lions if they will, my stomach is for gentler meat."

They returned to their line, leaving Jehiel to his work, assisted by one of the villagers. But for the rest of that day, Zabud remained so close to Solomon as sometimes to tread upon his heels.

At evening, the party made camp at Adoraim, where there was a small village. They built fires at the edge of the village and the people slaughtered two sheep, for which the princes paid. The pack mules carried bread and cheese, and good wine, which they mixed with sweet water from the well. Soon the smell of cooking and the sound of laughter and chatter rose against the stars.

Early enough, after supper was done, they rolled themselves in their cloaks and slept. But Solomon was restless; he slipped away from the fires and walked out alone, past the sheepfolds of the village into the open land. He wished that he had brought his lyre with him on this journey. A song was stirring in his mind, and his fingers moved restlessly as if across the strings.

> Thou makest darkness and it becomes night,
> In which all the beasts of the forest prowl.

The mood of the morning returned to him as he breathed deep of the cool, sweet air.

> How many are thy works, O Lord!
> In wisdom hast thou made them all.
> The earth is full of thy creations.

He heard, in imagination, the subtle combination of chords that would accompany this song, and he smiled into the night, knowing that few would ever hear it. For his songs were for himself alone; not even his mother had heard more than one or two. How should the son of the king rival the king? David, the sweet singer, whose lute and music had been the best in all the land, could not be equaled by his son's poor verses. It was true that Solomon performed excellently upon the eight-stringed lyre, but when sometimes his father called on him to sing and play, he chose either old songs or those David had written. Partly, this was because he knew it would give the old man great pleasure. But in part it was because Solomon did not like to be criticized, and in this matter he could hear, in imagination, his father saying, "My son, my son, remember that I wrote 'Why do you boast of evil, O mighty man!' when I was only a lad hiding in Adullam from the wrath of Saul, and therefore I know best how a song should go. Thus it should be constructed—this is awkward, this part limps . . ." and so on. All the faults seemed clear enough to Solomon's ears, but he could not bear that another should point them out to him—and of all others, certainly not his father. It was enough that he sang them to himself alone, out of his joy in God's creations. God heard them, and for whom else should a singer make a psalm?

A chill breeze sprang up, whispering among the juniper shrubs and piercing his woolen tunic. He turned back toward the camp, still sorting words and phrases in his mind, scarcely marking where he was going. As he drew near the flicker of a campfire, he heard low voices and stopped for a moment. He could make out two figures outlined against the light, and stepping a pace nearer saw, by the yellow glow that picked out noses and cheekbones, that one was his brother Adonijah and the other Nebat the Ephraimite.

He would have gone to sit with them, and perhaps share a cup of wine, but suddenly he heard Nebat say in a low voice but one which nevertheless carried clearly in the night, "But in truth, my cousin, there are many who think it would have been well if your arrow had fallen a pace or two short of the lion."

"You are a fool," Adonijah growled. "To what end?"

"Not so. My cousin is a fool. Or if he had not shouted a warning—"

"What do you say? It burst from me without thought. I cannot see a man threatened and stand still. What man can, unless he be made of iron?"

"All men know how great is the heart of my cousin. Yet, consider. None would have blamed you if the arrow shot from so far had struck Solomon. How many questions would have been answered with one simple answer: there is but one son of the king worthy of being anointed."

There was a brief silence. Then Adonijah rumbled, "I say this is folly. He has no wish to rule. In any case, I am the eldest."

Nebat's voice was softer, and smooth as oil. "As my cousin says, I am nothing. But I think he misjudges the desire of the king's wife, Bathsheba. Was she not his beloved, beyond all others? Was it not for her that the king placed the Hittite in the forefront of the battle, so that he was slain? Would he sin so desperately for my cousin's mother, Haggith, who now sits alone, old and silent, in the outer hall like a serving maid? The king is full of years, he will not live forever. Where, do you think, the lady Bathsheba is at this moment? At the side of the king—"

Adonijah chuckled. "If so, she must elbow aside the Shunammite girl, Abishag, who has so won my father's fancy."

"It may be that her elbows are readier than my cousin thinks."

Adonijah ceased from laughter, turning his head and resting one hand on his knee. "Go on. I am listening."

"Surely Joab, the captain of the host, must have told my cousin the rumors of the town? That Solomon has in his veins the blood of Benjamin, from his mother, and that if he were king the Lion of Benjamin might lie down with the Lamb of Judah? And so the tribe of Saul and that of David might be united. Thus do the people talk, setting you aside."

"No, by my hand. I never heard that. I have spoken with Joab—"

"Speak with him again, my cousin. Be master, in God's name," he said, playing upon the meaning of Adonijah's name, "and as for the son of Bathsheba, the peaceful one, let him soon find perfect peace in the grave."

Adonijah stretched out his arm and caught the other by the wrist. "Enough!" he said. "More than enough. Such words should not be spoken—not here, not now. When we return, I will see the captain of the host. Meantime, be silent, let us rest."

He rose and went to the fire.

Solomon, who had stood frozen in the darkness, stepped backward softly until he was some distance from the spot. Then only did he bury his face in his hands, stifling the sob that rose in his throat.

Let there be an end! he thought, bitterness twisting in his bowels. Amnon, my brother; Absalom, my brother. And now Adonijah! God of mercy, let me perish rather than be the cause of more grief and bloodshed.

He lifted his face to the glittering stars and the empty spaces between them. Before him swam the image of the lion, its eyes empty in death, blood clotting the fur of its mouth and mane. O God, he thought, let it not be an omen. Adonijah promised nothing, would hear no more, made his friend be silent. He, too, must remember the day of the sheep-shearing, the murder at Baal-hazor. Was it not he who held me in his arms that day? Did he not comfort me and stop my weeping, promising me his own toys, although he himself was white with terror? Did I not ride before him on his mule, on the Horonaim road, that the two of us might take courage from each other?

I have given him the lion's skin, he thought. I will give him the kingdom as well. If it must be an omen, let it not be of Israel divided, but of my end only.

And then at last he wept, for love of his brother and the fear of death.

Solomon slept little, but by morning he had mastered himself and appeared clear-eyed and serene. He breakfasted with his brother, eating curds and bread beside him and showing only a smiling face. He admired the pelt of the lion, which Jehiel proudly displayed, and offered milk from his own bowl to Nebat the Ephraimite.

It was while they ate that Zabud, who crouched behind Solomon to serve and pour out for him, touched him on the shoulder and said, "My lord, look yonder. Is that not too great a smoke for a shepherd's fire?"

Even as Solomon looked, Joel the son of Abner stood up and pointed. "If that is a cook-fire, it is an ugly breakfast. See the guests!"

On the horizon, a smudge of pale smoke rose high in the air, and above it wheeled dark specks, like flakes of ash—vultures balancing on wide pinions.

Adonijah sprang to his feet, wiping his hands on his kirtle. "You there," he called to one of the shepherds of the village, who stood shading his eyes and peering to the south. "What lies in that direction?"

"Only the village of Lahai-roi, which lies near the banks of the brook called Besor. It must be that which is burning, my lord."

"How far?"

"Less than an hour's journey."

Joel's nostrils dilated. "I can smell the burning. Bedouins! I would take an oath on it."

"They have raided before this, even as far as Beersheba and Ziklag," said the shepherd. "In my father's time they burned Ziklag to the ground, when David was lord of the city."

Already from the village came the cries of frightened women and the hoarse voices of the men. Adonijah turned to his armor-bearer. "Bring me my bow and my mount," he said.

"Does my brother mean to attack them alone?" asked Solomon. "Would it not be wiser for us to go to Beersheba and bring more men?"

Adonijah gave his loud, roaring laugh. "We are thirty here," he shouted. "The heroes of our father, the son of Jesse, were no more than thirty. Is my brother the lion-killer so soon dismayed? There cannot be many of the desert folk, or they would have struck at a walled town. Let us fall upon them and kill them before they can draw off with their booty."

The servants brought the horses and girded themselves to run, tightening their loincloths and discarding their tunics. The men swung into the saddle. At the last moment, some dozen of the villagers chose to go as well, armed with long knives and bronze-shod staves.

Zabud led up his master's steed. Solomon placed his hand on the saddle horn, looking through the rising dust at the preparations of his friends. They were without shields or swords, armed only with their hunting weapons: bows, javelins, throwing sticks, and daggers. Yet, perhaps they were as ready to go into battle as a host; they were young, high-hearted and eager, and they had abstained from women during the nine days of the hunt since leaving Jerusalem.

Then he thought: And if I am slain? Who can know the mind of Yahweh? It may be he has chosen this way for me, to resolve my doubts.

With that he mounted and took the javelins Zabud handed him. The armor-bearer, very pale, bestrode a sturdy little ass; he had never seen battle before, and he nervously and furtively dried the palms of his hands on the hem of his tunic.

Adonijah uttered a shrill whistle, and they set off at a gallop. Lahai-roi was an hour's journey on foot, but far less for mounted men; soon they could see the pale flames at the base of the smoke cloud, and then the dark shapes of men and camels. Still closer they rode, and they could see that the Bedouins had driven out all the villagers and their flocks and herds, and were trying to hasten them away. They could see the black beams outlined against flame, the clouds of sparks that soared upward when a roof collapsed. They heard yells, screams, and the frightened bleating of sheep.

There could be no doubt that the Bedouins had seen their approach, for now they detached themselves from their captives and rode out to meet the enemy. Without slackening his pace, Adonijah fitted an arrow to his bow; guiding his horse with his knees, he swerved to the side and shot. A camel stumbled with outstretched neck and fell awkwardly to its knees, pitching its rider headlong.

Solomon shouted the name of God. Behind him, others roared it: "Yahweh! God of Hosts!" Lances flew, burying themselves in the sandy soil.

The two groups met, mingled, became one. Solomon found himself beside a camel. He saw the red crescent of a sword swinging and evaded it. He flung a javelin upward, blindly, and the rider dove down upon him, his striped cloak spreading like a pair of wings. The weight of the man's body unhorsed Solomon. He rolled over and struggled to his feet. The two javelins which remained to him were gone, thrown from his grasp. He fumbled at his belt for his dagger; then he trod upon a man's hand and the hilt of a sword.

He snatched up the weapon. It was strange to the touch, being sickle-shaped and made of bronze, but he had little time to think of it, for a man on foot ran at him out of the dust cloud, with a spear gripped in both hands.

Solomon seized the spear by the shaft and pulled it toward him. Off balance, the man stumbled, and as he fell to his knees the prince leaped to one side and slashed at him.

There was slippery blood on the hands of Solomon, and sweat poured into his eyes. He stooped hastily to straighten the blade of the sword under his foot.

About him was a wild confusion in which were heard the neighing of horses and the snarls of men maddened by battle. Open mouths, clutching hands, the heads of camels, the flash of weapons emerged from the dust that filled the air. He saw that Zabud stood behind him, a dagger in one hand and the stump of a lance in the other, clutched like a sword. The front of his tunic was torn and his eyes glittered in a mask of dust and blood. A moment they panted at each other, then Solomon turned, knowing that his back was guarded, and plunged again into the mêlée.

Matters would have gone ill with the men of Israel, for they were outnumbered and lightly armed. But first, the villagers of Lahai-roi, when battle was joined, finding themselves unguarded, had caught up stones and sticks and rushed against their captors from the rear. Some armed themselves from the fallen and ran beneath the camels to slit their bellies; others, with their long shepherds' crooks, reached up to drag the desert men from their saddles, or thrust the staves between the camels' legs to trip them.

Then, as the fight swayed in the balance, the Simeonites of Adoraim, together with the running servants and those of the hunting party who had been mounted on slower beasts and so had dropped behind, now came up and fell upon the desert folk. This straw was enough. Such of the Bedouins as were still mounted turned their camels' heads to the south and fled away. The rest were slain or made captive.

But there remained six who would not surrender but stood back to back, their round shields before them, their swords still ready for combat. The men of Israel surrounded them grimly and in silence, and some were raising their bows to shoot when Solomon, tying a strip of cloth over a slight cut on his arm, pushed his way to the forefront.

"Hold your hands," he said. "These are not the sons of the Moon God."

Unlike the Bedouins, the six wore long straight gray tunics, brazen belts, and helmets of brass.

"What is your land?" Solomon asked.

One of the six, shorter of stature than his fellows and wearing a heavy gold neck-chain from which hung an enameled pendant, said, "We are Shebans, jackal of Israel."

Adonijah, leaning on his bow, put in impatiently, "What matter who they are, my brother? Since they stand on the side of our enemies, let us put them to death."

"It is true, their manners are not good," Solomon said mildly. "Nevertheless, I am curious. I have heard of Sheba, which is called the land of spices."

"You will hear more of it," said the leader of the Shebans truculently. "Others have heard of it. Know, Israelite, that we will not surrender but will fight to the death. Therefore, let us depart, or we will slay five of you for every one of us."

Adonijah burst into a bellow of laughter. "Yahweh protect me from the wrath of this little man," he cried.

"Nevertheless," said Solomon, "he has a large heart. Foolish the Shebans may be, but they are brave."

"Do you mock me?" The leader of the Shebans grinned with fury. "I will fight you hand to hand. Both of you at one time. By Ilmuqa, draw and come on!"

He took a step, shaking off the hand of one of his followers. At the same time, a throwing stick whirred from somewhere behind Solomon. It struck the front of the Sheban's helmet with a clang. The warrior pitched forward to the ground without another word.

Adonijah lifted his bow. "He who wishes to be spitted like a quail, let him raise his weapon," he said.

The other Shebans glanced at each other, and at their fallen leader. Then, in spite of his bold words, they threw down their swords and shields and surrendered.

Solomon bent over the man on the ground and removed his helmet. He was not dead; he would bear a lump like a pigeon's egg over one eye, but that was all. Without his helmet he could be seen to be a youth of about Solomon's age or a little younger. He had a pointed beard, trimmed small, and even unconscious as he was, his face had an impudent and cocky look.

Zabud stood at Solomon's side. He was full of elation and swaggered a little, for he had slain a man and felt exceedingly warlike. Solomon bade him make a litter of a cloak and two spears, and between them they carried the young Sheban down to the cool shade of trees near the banks of the stream where the rest of the wounded had been taken.

Solomon first washed himself of the grime of battle. Then he bathed the temples and face of the Sheban until the youth opened his eyes and struggled up on his elbow.

"Am I not dead?" he whispered, looking about dazedly. "I am shamed forever."

"It is no shame to be alive," Solomon said gently.

The other stared at him. "Ah, I remember you. How is it with my men? Did they die with their swords in their hands?"

"They are alive and unharmed."

The Sheban sighed, and lay back. "Who can trust servants?" he groaned. "Ah—my head! Would I were dead."

"Come," said Solomon. "Is it so great a burden to be alive? Sit up, drink some wine. You may fight to the death another day."

He motioned to Zabud, who put an arm under the Sheban and helped him to a sitting position.

"Tell me, what is your name?" Solomon asked.

"I am Sittar the son of Merisamis. My sister is Balkis, queen of the land of Sheba. And how shall I ever hold up my head—to be taken captive by an Israelite shepherd."

"Then be comforted," Solomon said drily. "For I am Solomon the son of David, who is king over Israel and Judah."

Sittar at once looked more cheerful. "Is it so?" he said. "Ah . . . then give me some wine."

He drank thirstily, and Solomon said, "Surely the land of Sheba is many days' journey to the south. How does the son of Merisamis come to be here? And with a raiding party of the desert men? Better to have come in peace, in the state that befits the brother of a queen, or if you must have war then at the head of many chariots and men."

"By Ilmuqa," said Sittar, grinning, "the voice is the voice of a stranger, but the words are those of my sister. So would she scold—she is more motherly to me than our mother herself."

Solomon could not repress a chuckle. "Was it to flee from her that you came?"

The young man returned his mirthful look. "No, no. We came to Egypt as wedding guests, for the Pharaoh Psusennes gave his wife's sister as wife to Hadad the Edomite, who is Pharaoh's friend. Afterwards, while we sat with Hadad one day, he told us of the many wrongs the Israelites had done to his people, and particularly of how the commander of their host, one Joab, whose name he cursed, had overcome the Edomites in battle and had remained six months in the

kingdom slaying every male, from the oldest to the youngest. But
Hadad and some of the servants of his father, the king, fled away
into Egypt and settled at the court of Pharaoh. Hadad said to us,
'I know that David is now old and dying, and Joab is old, and I will
stir up trouble against the dogs of Israel, to send their old age down
with blood.'

"He further said that he would send a message to one of the chieftains of the desert folk, who was once his father's friend, to see if a
raid might not be sent into Israel. Then it seemed to me a pleasant
adventure to bear this message and maybe go with the raiding party
to see how the Israelites fought. They fight well," he added, with a
comical grimace. "At first, my sister spoke against this, but the more
she did so, the more my heart became set on it, and at last she let
me go."

"The sister of Sittar is wise," said Solomon.

"Yes, she is wise."

"And is she an old woman?"

"No, no. She is very fair and young. In our land there is no king
but only a queen, who rules in the name of Samis, the Sun Goddess,
and my sister received the throne from our mother last year."

"I will meet with the sister of my friend one day," Solomon murmured. "And certainly I will send you back to her, that the first year
of her reign be not marked with mourning. But now that we are at
peace, will you not come back with me as a guest into my own country, to the city of Jerusalem, and stay with me for a time as a prince
should?"

Sittar said, "The men of Israel are noble warriors, generous captors,
and—their wine is good." He held out a hand, which Solomon
clasped. "How should I not come?"

Adonijah, who had been looking to the wounded, strode up accompanied by Joel the son of Abner, and by the moon-faced young
man, Adriel, who had been taking count of the dead.

"Yahweh was with us," said Adriel, snapping his fingers, "for there
are twenty of the sons of the Moon God killed, together with one of
the strangers, and many camels taken with their gear. Of our people
only seven were slain, three of them men of the village. However,
we have eight or nine hurt, some of them badly."

"We have no physician with us," Adonijah said. "What does my
brother think?"

"Let us make litters to carry the wounded," said Solomon. "We
will go to Beersheba, where there is a physician. As for the camels,

let us give them to the folk of Lahai-roi to requite them for the loss of their homes."

Adonijah frowned. "And what of this Sheban and his followers?"

"I have made peace with him," said Solomon, rising. "He is the son of a queen and the brother of a queen. He will come with us as a guest."

"My brother is open-handed," Adonijah growled.

"See, now," said Solomon, "little good would it do us to have his sister come seeking vengeance with an army for her brother's life. He will return home as a friend."

Adonijah shrugged. "Let my brother answer for it if any complain that this friend slew Israelites."

"I will do that."

They went to work, making litters to sling between pairs of horses or mules for the four wounded who could not ride. The people of Lahai-roi received the camels with gratitude, and some went with the men of Adoraim to their village to trade for tents and flour, while the others scratched in the ruins of the village to see if anything had escaped the fire. When all had rested and eaten, the two princes set out with their own folk to journey to Beersheba.

This was a strong town, well walled and armed since it lay upon the borders of the desert, and here the party found lodging, comfort for the hurt, and burial for one that had died on the way. Yet they did not rest long in Beersheba, for on the morning of the second day a courier came to them from Jerusalem. He had followed them from En Rimmon to Adoraim, thence to burned Lahai-roi and to Beersheba, without pause or refreshment save what he could snatch on the way.

He cast himself at the feet of the brothers. "My lords," he said, "I was commanded to tell you to return to Jerusalem without delay. By the will of God, the king your father lies very close to death."

For a brief instant the eyes of the brothers met. A single, stabbing glance passed between them. Then Solomon bent and lifted the messenger to his feet.

"Go, eat, drink, and sleep," he said. "You have done your work. Our feet are already upon the road."

# II THE ANOINTED

The palace of the king was hushed; in the hall, men talked in whispers and servants went to and fro on soft feet, for the king had been stricken at his dinner, had fallen upon the table like a dead man, had been lifted and carried to his bed, and there he had lain for three days unable to move more than his head and one hand.

Near a window that looked out upon the garden sat Joab the son of Zeruiah, commander of the host. A staff of olivewood bound with silver rings stood upright between his knees, and he tossed it gently from one hand to the other. His brown old face, webbed with fine wrinkles, the face of an Ishmaelite, was set masklike in crafty, secretive lines. It bore a faintly amused expression; from beneath heavy lids he seemed to look at the floor but watched the man across the room.

Benaiah the son of Jehoiada wore sword and dagger as befitted the captain of the king's bodyguard. He was a little past the middle age, but still powerful and unbent. He had once, armed only with a dagger, slain a lion in a pit where it had been trapped, and the shiny white weals that the claws had left on him were almost lost among the countless scars of his battles. Open as the sky was his broad-browed face, simple, good, and incapable of malice, showing nothing but anguish at the king's illness.

"If I could but take his pain on myself," he repeated, to one of the king's counselors, who stood beside him. "As I have taken blows for him in combat, would that Yahweh might let me now bear his pain."

"Peace," said the counselor, whose name was Chimham the son of

Barzillai. Slowly he stroked his curling white beard, which rippled over his chest like a breastplate of fleeces. "There is one agony every man must suffer for himself." And he added, indicating Joab with raised eyebrows, "There is one at least who does not seem to suffer."

Joab caught these words, softly as they were uttered. Slowly he got to his feet, supporting himself on the olivewood staff, and came close to Chimham. "Where is the need for grief?" he said. "Does the son of Barzillai hint that the king is dead?"

"No, no. I never said such a thing," Chimham replied, drawing himself a little away.

"Do I not know how quickly you ran to the king with lentils and bread when his son Absalom revolted against him? Yet where were the sons of Barzillai upon the day of battle? I saw you not in the forest of Ephraim."

"My lords—" Benaiah broke in.

The son of Zeruiah glanced at him and turned again to Chimham. In a lower voice, he said, "Go, you dead dog. I know these false tears and outcries. If you would know my grief, come to me in private."

Chimham pulled his robe about him and strove to speak calmly, although his voice trembled. "This is seemly talk—oh, seemly indeed! And from one who has been turned away from the king's presence before this for his misdeeds. Who was it beguiled Amasa with fair words and then thrust him in with a dagger? And slew Absalom in despite of the king's wishes? And who even now encourages that rough young man, Adonijah, and exalts him and whispers his praises? There are many who think you hope to make yourself secure in his kingship. But the fool rushes to his folly."

Joab remained calm as ever. The thick eyelids sank a trifle, veiling his eyes, and he said in a voice full of menace, "Let the son of Barzillai not make an enemy of me. If I slew those you speak of, how much less shall I account the slaying of a counselor of the king?"

Chimham looked once at the impassive Bedouin face, and departed without another word. Benaiah had risen, and he touched Joab on the arm.

"This was not like the captain of the host," he said reproachfully. "To put shame on an old man—"

"He is younger than I," said Joab, with a bitter smile. "He parades his age to win him respect. Ah—these sage old men whose mouths are full of platitudes as a pomegranate of seeds . . . there is no wisdom in them, only a stock of threadbare phrases which they repeat as a countrywoman recites magical incantations to avert the anger of a *baal* from her cattle. I will not be such a one. I was not made for counseling but for deeds."

"Tell me," said Benaiah, looking earnestly at him, "was it true what the son of Barzillai said? I mean, that you hope to make Adonijah king?"

"What? Does the son of Jehoiada believe such a thing?"

"I can only speak plainly. The captain knows I have no skill with fine words. It seems to me that no man should exalt one prince over another. It is for our lord the king to say who shall rule after him."

Joab opened his eyes very wide. He took Benaiah by both arms and said earnestly, "I am with my friend in this. May Yahweh smite me if I believe otherwise."

"Is it truth?"

"How can you doubt me? Have I ever lied to the son of Jehoiada? Wherever he has raged against the king's enemies, have I not been beside him? If he has been the king's shield, I have been his sword. How should I raise up one prince against another? If I slew Absalom," said Joab, his eyes filling with tears, "it was because he wished to make himself king in our lord's place. It is as you say: the king alone must bestow the crown of Israel."

Benaiah's face cleared. "I am gladdened by these words," he said. "There is no profit for Israel in division."

Joab nodded. Then he turned away as the far door swung open. "Ah," he said, "the lady Bathsheba has brought the two princes."

Solomon and Adonijah came into the hall. They had bathed and put on fresh clothes—blue linen shirts and fringed kirtles. With them came Solomon's mother, Bathsheba, a regal woman, though of small size, with an imperious eye. She wore no jewelry or gauds; plain and severe was her dress of pleated byssus dyed dark blue, and her long hair, still only a little gray, was braided under a thin veil.

"Do not tarry, you have tarried long enough on the way," she said sharply. "You need greet no one. Go directly up to the king's chamber. I will come at once. Ahishar!"

The steward of the house approached her, and bowed.

"Let me see the count of all who will sit down to dinner with us." She put back her veil, and nodded to Benaiah. She looked full at Joab, and said, "I am certain the captain of the host has far too much to do. We will not press him to stay."

Joab leaned with both hands on his stick. "As the lady Bathsheba says, I have many demands on me. For do I not watch over the safety of the kingdom?"

"Watch, then," she replied haughtily. "But let the son of Zeruiah not forget that he is the king's servant."

With that, she passed up the stair behind the two young men.

David the king lay against two pillows, staring at a shaft of sunlight which struck down from the open window. Palm fronds rustled outside, and he could hear the mourning of doves. The sweet smell of fresh earth breathed from the garden blended with a faint fragrance of cinnamon in the room—cassia, perfuming the garments of the maiden who sat beside his bed and held his hand in hers.

We are motes of dust, he thought, and tried to lift his left hand as if to brush it through the sunbeam. No, I had forgotten, I have no strength left. Where is the hand that smote the Philistine?

The girl felt the quiver of his attempted movement. "Does my lord wish for something?" she asked. "Some water?"

"No, nothing."

"Let me at least close the shutter. It grows chill."

He smiled weakly. "Abishag, Abishag. Let me feel that chill a little longer—it is the chill of life."

She was silent, her shoulders drooping.

"Do not think of death, my child," he said, "but rather of my life which has been long and full."

A lock of her hair fell across her eyes, resting lightly on her round, soft cheek. Maiden, he thought, how many summers have you left, before you, too, lie in the embrace of death? Will there be one to warm you when you are old, as you have lain beside me to warm me? Alas, why do I not depart now so that she may take her place among the living once more?

She had been sent with rejoicing from her village, with waving of green branches and with songs, to minister to the king, to lie on his bosom and keep the warmth of life in him, according to the directions of his physician. For her it was a holy task, for the spirit of Yahweh rested on David, so that she was like a handmaiden to God in her own thoughts. In the king's household she went about quietly, keeping her own counsel, tolerated by the other wives except Bathsheba, who felt her to be a usurper. But between her and the king had grown up such a love as there might be between pure lovers; to his frame she gave her bright vitality, and from him drew something of the holy power that had made him ruler.

David's eyes turned to the doorway. His sons entered, softly and hesitantly. Seeing them, tall and strong, he felt a stab of regret. I have not been such a father to them as I might. I have not readied them for kingship. If children might know all that their parents desire for them . . .

Adonijah, bearded and tanned, rough as the hills of Hebron from which his mother came, kissed the king's hand.

I have let him go unrestrained, thought David. I have not let him feel my wrath, so that he is now wayward and impetuous, yet easily led by others. His looks are royal, but he knows nothing save war and the chase, eating and drinking with his companions. Will he not give ear to any voice stronger than his? He is very like Absalom . . . too like him, and too dear to me to have been chided in season.

He looked at Solomon, slighter, quieter, more graceful. But also more withdrawn, so that if Adonijah's soul lay open to his father's eyes, that of Solomon was often shrouded in secrecy. He has the making of a wise man in him, David thought, and gentleness and mercy as well. But if the Philistines should come forth again, or enemies rise up out of Edom, can this mild youth lead an army? Can he stretch out his arm in judgment over all my people?

And behind Solomon was Bathsheba, who had no eyes for the dying king but only for her son. He felt a spasm of jealous irritation. Woman, he thought, you have already forgotten the sin that I committed for your sake, the death of your first husband, the death of our first child born of that sin. You turned away from me long ago; you will not be content to sit at my side, now, but must be about your son who is the hope of your heart.

The two princes stood at his bedside, and the king moved his hand slightly, looking at Adonijah. If I can bring these two together, he said to himself, so that between them they may hold the kingdom. If I had so wrought between my sons Absalom and Amnon that they could have been friends, then both might be alive today.

"Adonijah, my son," he said. "Watch over your brother."

The prince bowed his head. Bathsheba had tightened her lips so that deep, grooved lines ran from the corners of her mouth.

Now she is displeased, the king thought. As always, if I show affection for any other. For the sake of the love he had once had for her, and to keep the peace, he said, "Go now. But let Solomon remain and play for me, for it will soothe me. Abishag, bring the lyre."

The smile had come back to Bathsheba's face. She touched the coverlet lightly, where the king's feet made a hillock. Then she departed, with Adonijah behind her.

Abishag opened a chest and took out an eight-stringed lyre wrapped in Egyptian linen. She brought it to Solomon, who sat down at the foot of the bed. When she handed it to him her fingers brushed his, and the king did not fail to see the delicate blush that crept into her cheek. She bit her lip, turning hastily away, and sat down in a far corner.

Solomon tuned the lyre deftly. "What shall I play for my father?" he asked, drawing the plectrum lightly over the strings. "Jeduthun has sung a new song to the melody of 'The Dove of the Terebinths.' Will you hear it?"

Look at him, David thought, with his face half turned from me: what is he thinking? Why can I not see his heart?

Then he said abruptly, "Play one of your own songs for me, my son."

Solomon started. "My—my own? I have no songs."

"There is no musician who has not made at least one song of his own. Have you never composed even the smallest of verses?"

Solomon's fingers were white on the lyre. He shook his head.

"Look at me, my son," said David.

The prince raised his eyes with an effort.

"I am ready for death," said the king. "I have not long to listen."

His voice shook. Solomon bit his lips, staring at his father. All at once he saw, as he had not seen before, the wasted body, the scrawny neck and sunken cheeks, the dark hollows of the eyes as if charred by an inner fire. A great pity came over him for the help-lessness of the king, and mixed with it a wave of love for his father, sudden and irresistible.

He said, softly, "I am my father's servant." He cast through his mind, turning over his songs as a collector might finger carvings of ivory. He struck a chord or two, trying to decide what he might sing with the least fear of criticism, and then, almost without volition he found himself beginning that song which had come to him in the night, outside Adoraim:

> Let my whole being bless the Lord!
> O Lord, my God, thou art very great;
> Thou art robed with majesty and honor . . .
>
> How many are thy works, O Lord,
> In wisdom hast thou made them all.
> The earth is full of thy creations.

His voice grew stronger as he sang. He was no longer conscious of the old man, nor even of the girl with her disquietingly lovely face and the sweet scent of her skin.

He made the moon for fixed seasons;
The sun knows its time of setting.
He makes darkness and it becomes night
In which all the beasts of the forest prowl,
The young lions roaring after prey,
And seeking their food from God.
When the sun rises, they withdraw,
And crouch in their dens.
Man goes forth to his work,
And to his labor until evening . . .

May the glory of the Lord be forever!
May the Lord rejoice in his works.

David moved his head with an effort so that he could look both
at his son and at Abishag, who sat with her hands folded in her lap.
Her head was tilted a little on one side and there was a smile on her
mouth puckering one corner, a smile of pride and of wistfulness also.

So, the king said to himself, she looks on him with favor. Perhaps
because he has something of me in him. But as for him—does he see
her? The words of the Lord are still glorious for him; he has not
suffered enough. He has not yet learned the terrible sweetness of
desire and passion that must make a man of him. When I was his
age had I not won my wife with the bodies of a hundred Philistines?

Words of criticism sprang into his mind, thinking of the song, for
as a craftsman he could see its flaws leap out as clearly as black
sheep among white. But he checked himself from speaking, for he
had won, at least, this much: that Solomon had opened a tiny corner
of himself to his father.

"It is a splendid song, my son," he said, at last. "A good song. As
God sees me, it has not one fault."

When Adonijah came out of the palace, he found Joab waiting for
him beside the bronze gateway of the courtyard. The captain of the
host stopped him with a gesture, and said, "Will the son of Haggith
walk with me a little way? I have something to show him."

Adonijah said, "My chariot is here, and my friend Nebat waits for
me."

"Let him study patience, prince, and he will be the better for it."
Joab, holding the arm of the prince in his strong grip, led him
through the gate and into the street. They ascended a little way to
the corner, where the wall of the palace garden began. From here,
they could look down upon the flat roofs of the city sloping away

from them to the city wall far below, and the green Valley of Kidron beyond. The whitewashed houses shone in the sun, with here and there clumps of fig trees or almonds, or the feathery fronds of palms, and cutting among them, the deep cool shadows of streets.

"A fair city, my lord," said Joab. "A golden city, an excellent stronghold, fit for a king's seat."

Adonijah glanced sidelong at him. "Is it this you wished to show me?"

"What is there better for the son of Haggith to look upon? The city that may be his if he stretches out his hand to take it."

"Nebat the Ephraimite said that I should ask the captain of the host concerning my brother Solomon. That it is said if he were king, Benjamin and Judah would be united in him."

"It is what they say," Joab nodded.

"But he—he himself. Does he wish for the throne?"

"He is a weakling," said Joab, firmly. "I have seen him watching birds and beasts of the field. How can a lute-player be king?"

"My father was a lute-player."

"Your father . . ." Joab's voice changed, became almost tender. "He was a man. A man to be loved and followed. Have you never heard the tale of how Ishbaal, Eleazar, and Shammah brought him water? It was when we were in the cave of Adullam, penned in by the Philistines. David said, 'Oh, if someone would give me a drink of water now from the well beside the gate of Bethlehem!' Those three went out, then, and broke through the camp of the enemy and Ishbaal drew up water while the other two defended him. When they brought the water to David he wept for them, and he poured it out saying, 'God forbid that I should drink while others go thirsty. This is the blood of men who went at peril of their lives.' For such a man, Adonijah, one will dare many things."

"Yet you think Solomon a weakling? I saw him slaying Bedouins not four days since."

"He is a weakling," Joab repeated. "Let the son of Haggith remember that I also have seen something of war. Of all those men who fight well, how many are fit to lead an army? Only one in ten thousand has the right iron in him to give commands. Have you iron in you, Adonijah?"

He narrowed his eyes, peering like an eagle out over the city. "He does not wish for the throne, no. It is Bathsheba who will get it for him if she can. She has hated me, ever since she came into the house to be the bride of David. And she saw then that I was his right hand, I who stood beside him from the first, who was with him when he fled from Saul—I who have commanded the host for him for thirty years and more. She hates me—and I return it to her."

He laughed. "I took this city for my lord," he said, striking the street with his olivewood staff. "I climbed the hidden shaft from the spring of Gihon with fifty men, to open the gates. It was I who, finding Absalom caught in an oak, slew him with javelins so that he might not again threaten my dear lord. I slew Amasa, Absalom's captain, and Abner also, who would have made the son of Saul king in David's place. Do you not think my soul is heavy with blood, Adonijah? Yet I would do more than this . . . I served him long and lovingly, and now—" He turned on the prince, his voice low but sharp. "Now I would serve his son, since the king is all but dead."

"Yes . . . but Solomon is also his son," said Adonijah, uneasily. As always, when he spoke with Joab, he felt himself on the defensive, as if he were not quick enough to grasp everything that was said to him. The thought irritated him, and he continued more roughly, "Does Joab believe I shun the throne? All these hints come not to the heart of the matter. My father has not said which of us is to rule after him."

"Is there a question?" Joab said, with an impatient gesture. "The oldest son must be king, whatever the rabble may say. Let them speak of Solomon's fitness as much as they please, he is no more to me than are Chileab or Ithream. These are sons of the king also, but who considers them?"

"It may be so . . ."

Joab came a little closer. "Think, my lord. Did your father say nothing to you? Did he give you no sign, no indication of his will?"

Adonijah bit his fingernail. "Only that he wished for peace between Solomon and myself. 'Watch over your brother,' he said."

Joab's expression changed. "He said that?"

"A little while since, when I visited him."

"Then why do you hesitate?" Joab laughed aloud. " 'Watch over your brother.' What was that but the clear title of kingship? How better could he have said, 'You shall be king—and I leave Solomon in your charge'? Would he tell you to watch over your brother if Solomon were to be king, and you nothing?"

Adonijah lifted his head, looking over the city, his nostrils spread as if he would snuff it into himself like incense from an altar. "As God lives, it is true," he said. "Why did I not understand it?"

"You are modest, my lord, as befits you," said Joab, softly.

Adonijah gripped the son of Zeruiah by the arms. "Your eye is clearer than mine, old counselor," he said. "I will not forget your love when I have put on the crown. But there may be some who will quibble over the point, some who, as you have told me, believe Solomon should unite all Israel even though he does not wish it. Let us go down into the city and call together those who will be strongest for me, for when we have leaders the sheep will follow."

Joab took the prince's hand and touched it to his forehead, and kissed it. "Long live King Adonijah," he said. "Now do you speak like a king. Let us make haste, my lord, for we must speed quicker than other rumors. Your servant will call together those he is certain of, and we will at once proclaim your father's will."

"Come, then," said Adonijah. He turned to go, and already he walked with a heavier tread.

They went down into the city, to the house Adonijah kept for himself; it had belonged to his brother Absalom and was built of smooth limestone blocks and roofed with cedar. Here, Joab met with Nebat the Ephraimite, and Shisha the chief scribe, and Abiathar the high priest, and with several other wealthy men and counselors. He sent word also to some of the captains of thousands to join him, but only one of these, Eliam the son of Ahithophel, did so. Joab unfolded his mind to those who came, laying great emphasis on King David's words, "Watch over your brother," and upon the fact that Adonijah was the eldest, to whom should go the birthright, even as it had been in ancient times. And those who listened, while not wholly convinced, were swayed by the eloquence and reputation of Joab, but even more by the thought which Joab put into their heads, that they who first hailed the new king should be the first to taste the benefits of his gratitude.

In the end, all were agreed that Adonijah should be proclaimed. Chariots and horses were prepared, and runners were sent to invite Chileab and Ithream, the other sons of the king, and all the chief men and royal officials in the city, to come on the morrow to the ancient stone called the Stone of the Serpent. Adonijah gave orders to his steward to send sheep and oxen there for a sacrifice. Only Solomon was not invited, for Joab insisted that this might be interpreted as weakness on Adonijah's part. "In any case," he said, "when Bathsheba sees all is lost to her, she will take her son and leave the city."

On the following morning, the prince arrayed himself in his finest robes of scarlet and blue and gold. With fifty men riding before him, he went out of the city into the Valley of Kidron. There, below the Water Gate, lay the sacred spring of Gihon within its cave, and across the valley on a little eminence stood the Serpent's Stone, dark and pitted, immeasurably old, and bearing worn reliefs that could barely be made out on its surface: the coils of a serpent, a cup, a star, and the faint outline of a woman. Behind it was a flat place cut out of the hill, and here the servants of the prince built a fire and raised an altar of stones, and to this spot they drove the sheep and oxen for the sacrifice.

The city was in turmoil. Many gathered on the walls to watch the blue smoke ascend and the invited guests ride down to En-rogel. Many of those invited refused to attend; many of the townspeople spoke against Adonijah, saying that he was taking away the kingdom against his father's will, but others remembered him as good-hearted and generous. Some said he was another Absalom, and some shook their heads and said that this was the result of giving a young colt free rein, of never checking him by saying, "Why do you do thus and so?"

Through the midst of the buzzing crowds strode Nathan the prophet, tanned and angular, dressed in a single garment of stained and greasy leather. His lean arms and legs were the same color as this leather and of much the same texture. Before the mad glaze of his eyes men gave way, and whispers went up behind him: "He is going to see the king. Now we shall know."

But he did not go to the king. He entered the palace unchecked, and in the hall found Bathsheba with three of her handmaidens, embroidering cushions. She stood up as the prophet entered, and with a word to the maidens, went between the columns into the anteroom, beckoning Nathan to follow her.

"I have heard the noise and the shouting," she said. "What is it? Adonijah?"

He said harshly, and with none of the formal periphrasis that was polite, "You are right. Have you not heard that Adonijah has proclaimed himself king? Is this with the consent of our lord David?"

Her eyes flashed. "No. If he has done this thing it is of his own making."

"I think not. Adonijah has little will of his own. It is the jackal, Joab, who has misled this sheep. And the high priest, Abiathar, has thrown in with them."

Bathsheba swung away from him, clenching her fists. Her face was deathly pale. "Who else is with them?"

"They have invited the king's sons, and the royal officials of Judah, and many wealthy Benjamites, and they have sacrificed at the Serpent's Stone above En-rogel. But me they have not invited, nor the priest Zadok, nor Benaiah the captain of the bodyguard."

"The king's sons, you said? My son, also?"

"Not your son, Solomon."

"Oh, it is clear to me, clear as water," she said in a fury. "Thus does Joab tell me the moment of my death—that moment when Adonijah ascends the throne. But the king is not yet dead, nor is Adonijah yet crowned."

She faced the prophet, her back as straight as a young girl's. "There is a thing they do not know," she said. "My lord David promised me once that my son should be king after him."

"How was this?"

"It happened soon after Solomon was born, on a night in early summer. David came in to me and the child awoke and whimpered. He took the baby up and tossed it in the air, and kissed it, and said, 'Do not weep, my son. You will be king over all Israel.' I cast myself at his feet, and said, 'Let the son of Jesse remember this night. For if I grow old and ugly and withered and my lord turns from me, or if I should die and my son be raised by strangers, let my lord not turn him away, for the sake of the love we bear each other.' He said to me, 'I swear it, beloved. As God sees my love for you, your son shall be king after me.'"

Her voice had grown softer with memory, and her lips trembled. Nathan broke in, "That was long ago. Have you proof?"

"I need no proof. Yahweh heard his words and will confirm them. Come with me; let us go to the king."

Nathan took his beard in his hand. "Go in to him first, alone. I will come in after you as if from the city, and confirm your words. I would not have the king think this is something you and I planned behind his back."

Bathsheba went up to the king's chamber. The shutter of the window was closed, and Abishag sat as ever, holding David's hand. A clay lamp with three wicks fluttered nearby. Abishag looked up at the king's wife, then rose and bowed her head, moving a little away.

"My lord king," said Bathsheba, softly and urgently.

David opened his eyes. It was hard for him to see her in the dimness. He had not been asleep but remembering his youth, returning to it through the softness of Abishag's hand and the sweetness of her perfume. He had once again seen Bathsheba bathing in the sunlight on the flat roof of that house which still stood just below the palace; he had remembered her slenderness, her full breasts, the curve of her flank as she lightly laved herself with the perfumed water. He had seen her again in the gloom of the bedchamber—this very room—coming to him with love, with such desire and perfect will as matched his own. And now, opening his eyes he saw her still thus, and overlooked the wrinkles in her cheeks, the furrow that had grown between her brows, the coarseness that age had put about her lips and chin.

"Beloved," he said, but she was not listening. Instead, she had knelt beside the bed, saying, "My lord, hear me."

He sighed, moving his hand toward her. "Yes?"

"Does David remember a night when he came to me, when he lifted up the baby, Solomon, and promised me that the child should rule after him?"

He stirred, his daydream evaporating. "I promised that?"

"My lord, you swore to your maidservant by the Lord your God that Solomon should be king after you. It was in my chamber, on a night of the full moon, and I embraced your knees praying you to remember that night. And when you had sworn, later, you lay between my breasts and told me—"

Her voice broke. "Ah," she said, "that time has come which I feared on that very night, when I have become old and ugly and withered and my lord has forgotten me, and his son as well."

The words stirred a vague memory in his mind. Surely he had heard her say something of the sort, and on such a night as she described. But a husband and wife shared so many memories that all could not be remembered. Had he promised in truth? Or had he said something soothing, to allay her distress and bring her back to the frame of mind for love?

"What do you want?" he said.

She lifted an angry and woeful face to his. "Behold," she said, "Adonijah is king and you, my lord, do not know it. He has sacrificed oxen and sheep in abundance, and has invited all the sons of the king, but he has not invited Solomon your servant. Now, my lord, the eyes of all Israel are upon you, that you should tell them who shall sit on the throne of my lord the king after him. As it stands, the result will be that when my lord the king sleeps with his fathers, I and my son will be regarded as rebels."

She had barely finished speaking when Nathan entered. He came in swiftly, knelt down and touched the floor with his forehead, somehow making the obeisance seem perfunctory. He stood, and said in a voice that he strove to make soft, although from speaking to the people in the open it was naturally resonant and powerful, "My lord king, have you said, 'Adonijah shall be king after me'?"

David felt a rush of irritation for this man, who, prophet though he was, never seemed to address him with anything but rebuke. He rolled his head, looking to Abishag, and said, "Lift me up."

"He has gone down today to En-rogel," Nathan continued, quite forgetting to keep his voice low. "He has invited Joab—or, it may be, Joab invited him. And Abiathar the high priest is there, and many of the royal officials, and they are eating and drinking before him, and have said, 'Long live King Adonijah!' But me, your servant, and Zadok the priest, and Benaiah the son of Jehoiada, and Solomon your son they have not invited. Has this thing been brought about by my lord King David, and you have not told your servants that Adonijah should sit upon your throne after you?"

"Enough," said the king, in a voice which held the shadow of his former strength. The beating of his heart shook his whole body, and he clenched his teeth to hold in his rage and anguish. Behind his back both sides had plotted and schemed, each laying their own snares. But no choice was left him, for it was clear Adonijah was only the tool of Joab in this matter, and it was equally clear to him that he could not permit what was nothing more than the same act of rebellion as Absalom's. Adonijah had flouted him, had gone from his very bedside thinking the king was too weak and old to withstand him, and had proclaimed himself. Besides, perhaps he *had* promised Bathsheba . . .

He said, "Go, call for me Zadok the priest, and Benaiah the captain of my bodyguard, and also my scribe, Shisha."

"He is with Adonijah," growled Nathan.

"Then call to me Jehoshaphat the recorder, that he may be my scribe for now."

With a bow that was scarcely more than a nod, the prophet left the room. David glanced up at Abishag and saw that tears stood in her eyes, but that she was nodding at him. He said to his wife, "Bathsheba, as the Lord lives who has ransomed my life out of adversity, as I swore to you once by the God of Israel that your son should be king after me, so will I do this day."

She bowed her head, but she could not hide the quick smile of triumph that lighted her face. "My lord king, live forever," she said, repeating the formula without thinking of its meaning.

Solomon and the young prince of Sheba sat in the highest chamber of the palace, a large airy room with limed walls, and windows that looked north over the suburbs of the city toward the distant folded hills. The room was cool and clean, and very simply furnished: there were a few painted chests in which rolls of books and writing implements were kept, and drawn close to the windows, a folding table and two cushioned chairs without backs. Clay pots of fresh flowers stood all about lending warm color to the austere walls.

The two were idly playing the Egyptian game of cones and pyramids. Sittar twirled the square top and cast it on the ivory board.

"Three!" he said. "Luck stands with me."

Solomon stretched his legs out, resting his hands on his thighs. "Luck . . ." he said. "I am not lucky, son of Merisamis. I rarely win at games."

Sittar chuckled. "This is small luck. My uncle, the respected and solemn priest Yadiel, tells me that the only luck is to be beloved of the gods. But I have another way of thinking: to be beloved of women, and to be lucky in battle. *I* was not so lucky this time," he added, ruefully.

It was the first time since his surrender that he had mentioned his defeat. Solomon looked at him with affection.

"Now, why does my cousin still mourn for what is done? Let us pretend Sittar came with a caravan of camels and spices, and that we met and embraced peacefully. However it happened, it was good that we met."

He touched the other's arm.

"My cousin is right," Sittar said. He was too lively and volatile to remain downcast for long. "In any case, when I return to Egypt I will tell my sister that I was only taken after I slew a hundred Israelites."

He scowled in mock ferocity, then opened his eyes very wide as if astonished at his own lie. Solomon burst out laughing, and Sittar joined him.

"If my cousin wishes, I can give him trophies," Solomon said. "Or proofs—a letter explaining that it was he who took me captive, for instance."

He got up and went to a chest on which stood a long-necked pitcher of cool wine and a dish of dates. He poured two cups of wine and gave one to Sittar.

"Indeed," he said, "my cousin has taken me captive. I have not felt so light-hearted in many days."

After leaving his father's bedside the day before, he had joined Sittar and taken him in his chariot through the city and about its suburbs, to point out its beauties. They had dined together, and Sittar had won even Bathsheba's heart with his wit and his manners. All that night they had been together, first talking on the rooftop under the stars, then in Solomon's bedchamber, then in Sittar's; then creeping down in the middle night, when all were asleep, to scour the kitchen, and then whispering in the garden with bread and cheese, fruit and wine—the spoils of their raid—and at last, yawning and silly, light-headed from too much drink and too many confidences, they had fallen asleep on the floor of this high room with the city gray in the morning below them.

Sittar was a blend of frivolity and earnestness, sometimes boasting of his great deeds, sometimes jesting madly, and then recalling soberly the many places he had visited and the problems his sister faced in the government of their land. Again and again, his talk came back to her: she was wise, she was foolish, she pestered Sittar but he adored her. She could be gracious and guileful at once, she had outwitted her counselors in many matters, she had taken the throne when all thought her too young and had won the respect even of her enemies. The people worshipped her, not only because she was the embodiment of Shams, the Light of Heaven, but because she was all good things to them: their own daughters, wives, and lovers in her one person.

And now Sittar said suddenly, "I, too, have been happy with my cousin. Listen—why does not Solomon return with me to Egypt, to meet my sister?"

He sprang up and strode about restlessly. "An idea worthy of my mother's son! What is to hinder you? Come! You will fall in love with my sister as does every man who meets her. We shall be brothers; you will become her consort, priest of Ilmuqa.

"Ah, but I forgot," he added, "your God would be angry, for I have heard how jealous he is."

"That priesthood is not for me," Solomon laughed. "But then, I need not wed your sister, only meet her."

"Oh, her heart would be drawn to Solomon. She is like my cousin in many ways. She, too, watches the beasts and birds, and will go sometimes into the hills alone, riding her white horse which the Pharaoh sent her when she was crowned. And like my cousin she reads much—books, books, of paper and parchment. I could not keep a tithe of it in my head."

Solomon leaned against the casement of a window, staring out at the sky, tapping the wine cup with a fingernail. "Why not?" he said. "Why should I not go?"

Sittar came behind him, clapping him on the shoulder joyfully. "Pharaoh will provide for us," he said. "We will make his kingdom our table. If my sister wearies Solomon with her queenly talk, we will find some of those high-breasted Egyptian maidens with long lashes, eyes like does, and clever fingers . . . eh? Then, in a month perhaps, we will go in our boats down the Red Sea and so home. You will see Marib, the city of incense—all those things of which I told you last night. And I will find my cousin a little dove of Almakah who will content him so that he will never go home again."

Solomon turned, looking into his friend's happy face. "You are a madman, my cousin," he said, clasping Sittar by both arms. "Must we go this very instant? Or can I not show you some of my own land first? We have maidens here as well. The girls of Judah are very fair, and there are Shunammites who . . . who are said to be—"

He paused. Sittar said, "Oh, I see where my cousin's heart lies. Did I not hear that word last night once or twice: the maids of Shunem are like gazelles, and so on? Be it so. Let me remain a week, and then come with me. Will you do so?"

"By my hand, I will!"

"A bargain! We must seal it in wine."

They slapped their hands together like a pair of merchants and Solomon turned to get the pitcher. As he did so, Benaiah came suddenly into the room. He came directly to Solomon, knelt, and made obeisance.

"My lord," he said. "Live forever."

Solomon stood frozen. Neither the significance of this act, nor the words of the captain of the bodyguard penetrated his mind. He could only think that his father was dead and that Benaiah was prostrating himself in grief.

Benaiah rose to his feet, and went on, "It is the will of my lord David that his son Solomon come before him, to receive the throne of Israel."

A wave of nausea swept over Solomon. His pulses tolled in his ears and sweat started out upon his body. His mind shrank from the words: the throne of Israel. They contained the awful power of decision, choices, authority, and the dreadful loneliness of kingship, falling on him like an immense mantle, gorgeous with gold but weighty to be worn.

He said, "The captain must be mistaken. Not I."

There was no answer. He saw the hands of the captain, hairy and capable, the tiles of the floor dusty with footprints, the astonishment in the eyes of Sittar.

I am alone, now, he thought. And Adonijah?—for the conversation he had overheard in the darkness at Adoraim returned to him and he saw now that the Ephraimite had been right. His mother, Bathsheba, had so wrought that the dying old man had given him the

crown. I will go to my father, he said to himself, and tell him I will
not have it. I am not worthy . . . But even as the thought crossed
his mind he knew it to be untrue and thrust it away. He had wanted
the kingship always; who could resist such a gift?

Benaiah was watching him. Solomon drew a breath, and said, "Let
us go to the king." His first step was unsteady, then he controlled
himself and went firmly to the door.

The king's chamber was crowded. Jehoshaphat the recorder sat
upon the floor writing on a waxed tablet, his pointed beard moving
steadily as he shaped the words unconsciously with his lips. Bathsheba stood under the window. Zadok the priest was there, not yet
robed in his vestments for he had been called in haste, and Nathan
leaned upon his long staff with a look of sour satisfaction on his hard
features. Abishag stood forgotten and silent in a corner, but as Solomon entered, her eyes fastened on him, shining and tender, luminous
in the shadows.

Solomon did obeisance to the king. Anger at Adonijah's folly, annoyance at Bathsheba and Nathan, the knowledge of all the threads
gathered together that had been spinning behind his back during
the last year or more—these things had given David temporary
vigor. He was able to move his right hand a little more, and he raised
it, beckoning weakly to his son. Solomon rose. Words rushed into
his head—what would be fitting to say? To thank my father for re-
linquishing the throne? To thank him for dying? To say, I am going
to Egypt with Sittar, give my brother the throne . . . ?

David was already speaking. He said, "Cause Solomon my son
to ride upon my own mule, and bring him down to Gihon. Let Zadok
the priest anoint him there king over Israel. Then blow the trumpet
and say, 'Long live King Solomon!' You shall then go up behind him
and he shall come in and sit upon my throne and he shall be king
in my stead. Him do I command to be leader over Israel and Judah."

It seemed to Solomon that his father's voice was cold and remote,
that there was no love in this act. His knees shook, and he cried out
within himself, Father! Do not turn from me!

It was as if something of this mute cry was heard by the king.
His eyes softened, and in a gentler tone he said, "Go, my son. Be
strong and show yourself a man."

At this, the knot in Solomon's chest loosened. The tears sprang to
his eyes, blurring his father's face, but he held his back straight, and
his chin high.

Benaiah, at his right hand, said, "So be it! May Yahweh confirm
the words of my lord the king. As God has been with my lord, so

may he be with Solomon and make his throne greater than the throne of my lord King David."

They led Solomon from the chamber. He was bathed and perfumed, and his hair and beard combed. Then they put on him a tunic and kirtle of linen white as snow, and over it a long robe of purple, open in front like a pair of curved wings and striped above the hem with blue and white and gold. About his neck they put a broad golden collar; on his feet, sandals of gilded leather. A golden circlet set with precious stones—the crown David had taken out of Ammon—was placed on his head. He was brought into the courtyard where the bright sun made him blink. The servants had gone out to shout the tidings in the streets, and he could hear a confused, distant uproar as the news spread.

The white mule of King David was brought to him and he mounted. His shield-bearer, Zabud, held the bridle, looking up at him with awe, and in the wide eyes he saw mirrored not himself but the image of a king, terrible and beautiful, with the hand of God upon him. Once again, he felt dizziness sway him.

Benaiah had gone forth to call the king's bodyguard, and the street beyond the palace gate was already full of soldiers: Cherethites with heavy bows and javelins, and Pelethites with their long, straight swords shaped like arrowheads, each man with a horned helmet of brass and a round shield of ox hide studded with bronze. Nathan the prophet went before, and Zabud led the king's mule out through the gate followed by all those in the palace.

There was the thin music of flutes and the shaking of sistra, and then a great billowing wave of hosannas as the procession came out into the market place. All along the way flowers were strewn upon the street, and people leaned from the rooftops and from narrow windows to hail the new king. Solomon saw the hundreds of faces and waving arms as a bright blur, and the noise beat upon his ears like the crashing of a waterfall, endless and stunning.

They went out of the city and down to the pool of Gihon, across from En-rogel, where the smoke of Adonijah's sacrificial fires still went up, and the folk who were with him ceased their feasting to come and stare into the valley. A black tent had been set up beside the holy pool, and Zadok sat within it, wearing the checkered tunic and linen breeches, with a violet sash about his waist and a violet cap bound with a linen turban. As Solomon drew near, the priest stood up and went out to meet him. The armor-bearer helped Solomon dismount, and he knelt down beside the pool of Gihon. All the noise ceased as if an angel of the Lord had passed over the multitude. There was a deep silence over the valley and the city.

An acolyte brought a horn of oil from the tent. Zadok took it and poured it over Solomon's hair.

"The Lord God has anointed you to be ruler over his people, Israel," he said. He raised Solomon to his feet.

There came a great blast of trumpets, and all the people cried, "Long live King Solomon!" so that the earth shook.

Jonathan the son of Abiathar, the high priest, had run speedily up to the Serpent's Stone to tell the news. At once, all the supporters of Adonijah fled without excusing themselves; some went to their houses and others joined the throng below and tried to look as if they had been there from the first. As for Joab, he said to Adonijah, "Now the die is cast. Quick as we were, we were too slow. I do not think your brother will harm you, for he is a man of peace, but it may be that Benaiah the son of Jehoiada may fancy I have broken a certain promise I made him. I am therefore going to my estate in Bethlehem. Remember, son of Haggith, for the prudent man there is always another time, another day." With that he departed also, climbing up into the hills, followed by Nebat the Ephraimite and by the men of his own bodyguard.

He had been right. Benaiah had ascertained that the captains of thousands stood with Solomon, all save Eliam the son of Ahithophel, who was too proud to run away but sat in his house and waited for judgment. The king's bodyguard outnumbered by far all the armed men of Adonijah, and Benaiah sent a company of Pelethites up to the Serpent's Stone. They found Adonijah standing, between fury and doubt, among the broken meats of the feast, deserted by all save Jehiel his armor-bearer. They led him down to Gihon and brought him before the new king.

The brothers stood face to face, and Solomon said, "I will not have my brother think I mean him ill. Will Adonijah make peace with me?"

The son of Haggith, glowering, said in a grating voice, "Let the king do his will."

The weight which Solomon had felt upon his shoulders pressed more heavily upon him, and he knew that the first of his decisions was at hand, and that he must make it under the eyes of all the people. He said, in a soft voice, "I swear to you, as God lives, I did not seek the throne. Can we not love one another still, as brothers? Let it not be between us as it was between Amnon and Absalom."

Adonijah glared at him in silence.

"Very well," said Solomon, drawing himself up. "Let my brother remember that I *am* the king. If there is good in the son of Haggith, not a hair of him shall fall to the ground. But if evil be found in him, he shall die."

There blazed from his eyes a living fire. Adonijah saw that this was no longer his younger brother who stood before him, but a new man, the leader of Israel, utterly changed and enlarged by the power that was in him. He was shaken, and puzzled as well, for he was unaccustomed to independent thought save in such active sports as war and hunting. Then he recalled Joab's words: "There is always another day."

He said, sullenly, "I am the king's servant. Let there be peace between us."

Solomon embraced him. "Go to your house," he said. "If there was wrong done, it is forgotten."

With that, he turned away. Joyful shouts surrounded him, and on them he was carried to the palace, to sit upon the throne of his father.

# III  BALKIS

A few days later, Solomon took leave of Sittar. He gave his friend many rich presents, among them a sword of Philistine iron ornamented with gold, a belt richly decorated with gems, and a massy gold ring in which was set a jasper seal engraved with a many-pointed star. He gave him also money for the passage, and gifts for his sister. In exchange, the son of Merisamis gave the king his own dagger, hammered of iron that had fallen from the sky, with a hilt of silver encrusted with pearls.

"It is little enough to give to a king," he said, with his lively smile, "but my heart goes with it. Alas, I would not have my cousin lose his high estate, but I wish he could have come with me."

"It is my own wish," said Solomon. "But Yahweh has decreed otherwise. There will be a place ready for my friend whenever he chooses to visit me."

"I will come, and soon," Sittar promised.

Solomon sent chariots and horsemen to escort him and his five followers to the city of Gaza, from which they took ship for Egypt rather than ride the long coast road. The ship brought them to the city of Tanis where, in a cool and pleasant palace a little way up the river, Sittar's sister Balkis was lodged in state.

The queen had risen only a short time before, and had come from her bath when her brother was announced. She quickly drew on a striped robe pinned with a brooch on one shoulder and, abandoning ceremony, ran out to meet him. She threw her arms about him and then held him off and looked at him, shaking her still-damp hair out of her eyes.

"So you have returned, my young warrior," she said. "Let me see you. No wounds?"

"Only a bruise on the head, long healed. I promised to tell my sister that I had slain a hundred Israelites, but it is hopeless. I slew perhaps one, before I was taken."

"You were made captive?" She stared at him.

"I will tell you everything. But I have just come from the ship. In the name of Ilmuqa, does my sister never eat breakfast?"

She drew him by the hand to the terrace, where loaves of bread, honeycombs, and ripe figs were set out on silver dishes. He sat down and began eating, and with his mouth full told her the whole tale of his raid and his friendship with Solomon.

"I tell you, he is a man among a hundred thousand," he concluded, wiping his fingers on a napkin. "Full of grace, witty, thoughtful, tender, wise—I have not seen a man like him in our own country. How I wish he could have come with me! My sister would have lost her heart, as I have."

"Perhaps," said Balkis drily. "But a man loved by men is not always acceptable to women."

"Pooh! Does my sister think him one of the languishing Egyptian lords, scented and curled, who fondle boys? It is not so. I have seen him fight—by S'ahr, he is a lion. And yet he is no swaggering bully like his brother Adonijah. No, he is a man of peace. His very name means 'peaceful.' When we talked, he told me that his land has known nothing but wars with their neighbors. He has great plans— he will make Israel a rich and glorious nation."

She leaned back in her chair, resting her cheek on the back of one hand, studying his animated face. The sun, shining through the foliage of the tall date palms which ringed the garden, made her skin glow: it was the color of the honeycomb on the silver plate. Her dark, glossy hair, unbound, fell in ringlets below her shoulders. Ever and again, the waving palms passed shadows across her face so that her eyes seemed to move, but in fact, she had an unblinking regard, which helped to mask her feelings. Her eyes were large, round like a child's, of a curious deep violet color almost black, and utterly inscrutable.

She said, "He has made an Israelite out of my brother. Are there none who hate him?"

"He is beloved by all. You should have seen the people of the city when he was anointed. Only his brother Adonijah and those who supported him—and even them he put down—and Adonijah he won over so that he knelt at his brother's feet."

"Well, I am grateful to him," said Balkis. "Not only for sparing my brother's life, but for binding him so close in friendship. My brother's friend must be mine."

"Oh, you have other reasons for gratitude. He sent my sister gifts worthy of her state. The porters will bring them up from the ship."

He stretched his arms out, and yawned. "The air of Egypt is warmer and lazier than that of Jerusalem," he said. Then, with his elbows on the table, he added, "Sister, shall we not go to see Jerusalem when your visit here is done?"

She smiled fondly at him. "My brother is as restless as a caged leopard. Be patient! We shall go one day. You have but just returned. We must set out for home, Sittar. I have my own throne, my own country to govern. And our mother is very old; soon the Goddess will take her to herself, and we cannot be absent when that happens. I have been here too long already. My excuse has been that I have waited for my brother."

"Come, now," laughed Sittar. "My sister has surely spent her time well with diplomacy and courtly intrigues, financial matters, treaties and the like, such as are beyond my foolish understanding."

"It may be so," she said, dimpling. "Yet now we must return home." For all her lightness, he knew his sister well enough to recognize that the subject was closed. She stood up, smoothing her robe over her hips. "I will sacrifice to Shams in gratitude for my brother's safe return. And I will not forget to pray for the health of his friend, the king of Israel."

She left him to finish his breakfast, and went to place herself in the hands of her tiring-women, to be perfumed with myrrh, to have her hair dressed, her nails varnished with henna, her eyelids shadowed with lapis lazuli, her lips tinted, her body robed in queenly robes. She was expecting a visit that forenoon from Hadad the son of Hadar, who called himself king of Edom.

Sittar had, in fact, hit close to the truth: Balkis had spent her time well in Egypt, and yet not so profitably as she could have wished. When Sittar had expressed his desire to go with a raiding party, she had allowed him to do so because it did, in fact, give her an excuse for remaining in Egypt a little longer. She loved her brother no less, but she had early learned the first principle of statecraft: that the ruler has nothing that is his own.

The trade goods of the land of Sheba were spices, sweet-smelling herbs and tree-bark—for perfumes and ointments, for flavoring foods, and above all for the incense so necessary to the worship of the gods of every land. Balkis had negotiated sales with Pharaoh, but in addition she was concerned with the use of ports for shipment of her spices to the lands upon the Great Sea: to Crete, Phoenicia, Libya, and Chittim, and even farther places. But the distance was great—more than a hundred days northward by caravan to Egypt or Israel—and the risks were greater. Balkis wished to reduce her expenses as well as her risks. She was ambitious: her fertile, fragrant land had been wrested from the desert by irrigation ditches and dams, by long and difficult labor, and she saw its boundaries stretching further and further, its wealth and power growing—there was no limit to the horizon, so far as the Holy Sun might cast her life-giving beams. In that vision every man from her brother to Pharaoh himself was no more than a piece to be moved upon the board, a cone or a pyramid to be advanced or lost for the sake of the game.

When she was dressed, she went to a quiet chamber overlooking the river, to await Hadad. Her scribe accompanied her, sitting at her feet and taking down at her dictation letters to her officers and ministers ordering them to prepare for her return home. Before this work was done, Hadad was ushered in to her.

He had lived in Egypt since childhood, but in spite of his dress, his speech, and even the tight-curled chin beard bound with gold wires, he had a foreign look: the white linen coif framed a proud, bony face with high cheekbones, thin lips, and the deep-set far-watching eyes of a desert nomad. He had never forgotten that he was an exile; although Pharaoh had made him almost a son, had indeed linked him in marriage to the house of Taanau, yet he nursed his bitterness with miserly pleasure. He could remember nothing of the flight from Edom, and yet he had been told so many tales of the slaughter and the cruelty of the invading Israelites that he hated them as if he held clearly before his own eyes the spectacle of men butchered, children dashed to death, and weeping wives. Not even the beauty of the Sheban queen could distract him from his main purpose.

He bowed stiffly and made himself comfortable on a bench. Balkis dismissed her secretary, and turned to Hadad with a smile.

"The son of Hadar has surely heard the news," she said. "My brother Sittar has returned out of Israel."

"I met him in the hall below and spoke to him. It seems the raid was not successful."

"Lord Hadad must know," said Balkis, "that every raid is successful. The chief purpose of a raid is to distract an enemy, to goad him, to irritate him, to bleed him by little and little. If no more than a single man of the enemy has been killed, this purpose has been served. But forgive me," she added, looking demurely at the ground. "I have no need to instruct the son of Hadar in military matters."

"The queen is mistress of every art," replied Hadad. "In any case, the village of Lahai-roi was burned to ashes. I would I could see their whole land so served."

"My brother has told me of their new king. Solomon the son of David now reigns."

Hadad sat erect. "Is David then dead?"

"By this time it may be he is. He placed Solomon on the throne while he himself was yet alive, but he was ill and dying, so says Sittar."

"On the throne? Over the head of the son of Haggith?" Hadad plucked at his beard. "This is news indeed, and of great interest."

"How so? Does the son of Hadar know Solomon?"

"I have heard of him. His mother is Bathsheba, whose beauty was so great that King David wished to marry her, although she was already wedded to Uriah the Hittite, one of the king's captains. David instructed the commander of his host, the accursed Joab, to place the man in the forefront of battle and withdraw from him so that he might be slain. When this happened, the king took the woman."

"And Solomon is the child of that union?"

"Yes, but not the first child—that one died at birth. He is the second. And I have heard that he was so cherished and spoiled by his doting mother that he became a milksop, soft and peace-loving, pliant as a reed."

Balkis weighed this in her mind with what her brother had told her, but said nothing.

"Adonijah the son of Haggith, on the other hand, is the older of the two," Hadad went on. "He is reckless and violent, a brawler and a noted hunter. There are also Chileab and Ithream, but the first is weak-witted and the second a drunkard. Many felt sure Adonijah would gain the throne, for he is the eldest and has been greatly indulged by his father. Now let the queen tell me, is this not a condition ripe for hostility? May I not take advantage of it, somehow setting one brother against the other to divide the kingdom?"

He sprang to his feet in restless excitement. "Ha! If I could but throw them against each other. Then, while they quarrel, raise up my people in revolt, hurl in my armies and crush them, first one then the other. Edom in my hand! King of Edom!"

Balkis said softly, "Good. Where are your armies, son of Hadar?"

He deflated like a burst wineskin, and sank down on the bench again. "It may be that Pharaoh will loan men . . . chariots . . ."

His voice trailed away. Balkis studied him for a moment, and then said with every evidence of friendly warmth, "My sympathy goes out to my friend, the lord of Edom. But he deceives himself. I have spoken with my lord Psusennes on other matters, and I judge him to be as close-fisted as a Phoenician dye-merchant. His soul is thrifty. Furthermore, he dreams of the past, when Egypt was glorious, but his sinews are shrunken; he has no stomach for war. He will neither give nor loan soldiers . . . or so I think. But I am a child before the wisdom of Hadad."

The Edomite nodded glumly. "I have schooled myself to patience; I must wait a little longer. But if I could strike—*now*. I will return to Edom," he said, decisively. "I will draw together my own people, gather the chieftains, confer with the chiefs of the Bedouins, the Moabites also it may be . . ."

"How long will it take, do you think?"

"It is not easy to raise an army," he replied. "I must prove my lineage, find friends, negotiate with many men. A year, perhaps two years. And by then the opportunity may have vanished." He struck his hands together.

Balkis bent toward him. "Tell me, my lord, do you find me fair to look upon?" she asked.

He stared at her in surprise. The fine-textured thin robes clung to her figure, revealing the line of breast and thigh; the honey-colored flesh shone through the pale tints of the gauze. He opened his mouth, but before he could reply she said, "I am answered, I think. It may well be that the son of David will also find me fair."

He lifted his eyebrows. "What has this to do—?"

"May I counsel my friend Hadad? Then listen: go into Edom. Raise your army, equip it, prepare for war. When everything is ready send word to me. Then Sheba will go up against Israel."

"With soldiers?"

"With gifts. With friendly words and smiles."

"I do not understand."

She shrugged impatiently. "Hadad spoke of his opportunity vanishing. But I will make an opportunity. Do not the Edomites have a proverb: 'A well, a woman, a sword are breeders of discord'? I will go to Israel and destroy their king. I will breed discord between him and his brother so that Hadad may attack. And in return—"

She gathered a pleat of her skirt between her fingers, examining it thoughtfully. "The son of Hadar knows that when I send incense and spices and goldwork north, there is always danger of brigands attacking the caravans. And when I come to the seaports there are tolls and taxes to be paid, and shipping costs. I have spoken with Pharaoh. He denies me the sea, save at his profit. But in Philistia there are seaports such as Askelon and Gaza. And Israel is also the bridge by land to Phoenicia, Aram, and Asshur.

"My lord Hadad, when he is king of Edom, will guard at his own expense all my caravans. And he will guarantee me free passage to the sea, and passage without toll through all his land. This is all I ask."

He blew out a long breath of admiration. "The queen's demands are small indeed," he said ironically. "The worth of a thousand shekels on every caravan, at a rough estimate."

"Is it not the worth of a kingdom? Then Edom must indeed be small and poor. Still," she added, with an air of indifference, "it is all one to me. Let my friend deal with Pharaoh if he wishes."

Hadad shook his head. "No. It is acceptable. But by the eye of Ra, the queen Balkis drives a hard bargain. By the living Ra, I have not met the queen's match in statecraft in all my life. And it is said she has not yet seen twenty-two summers. What a land of wisdom must be Sheba!"

Balkis could not repress a smile before his obvious admiration. "Let me ask the son of Hadar, what did he do when he was a boy, when he came first to the court of Psusennes?"

He frowned. "When I was a boy? Why—I played with the sons of Pharaoh. What does the queen mean, to ask what games we played?"

"No. Only to hear that. But my lord, from the age of six years I was schooled in queenship. When I was chosen as my mother's successor, I was brought to the altar of Shams, and I began my training. For fifteen years I have learned what it is to rule. I had no childhood as other children have."

Her eyes had grown darker, her face somber. "Yet I am grateful for the good opinion of my friend, the son of Hadar. Now I will call the scribe that our contract may be drawn up in good form and sealed by us both."

She rose, and he also stood up and bowed. "One thing more," she said. "When I am in Jerusalem, and I judge all is ripe for Hadad's armies to attack, I will send him a token." She lifted a pendant that hung from a chain round her neck, a disk of gold bearing an image of the Sun Mother. "This will do. Look at it well, my lord, so that you will know it when next you see it."

He approached a few steps to examine the disk. She stared down at his bent head with her unblinking violet eyes, and thought to herself, Who can trust a king? When Hadad has done my fighting for me he may die, who knows? Even kings may be helped to die suddenly. And then his kingdom may pass under the hands of my servants so that our bargain be not a constant thorn in his side . . . or mine. If it be the will of the Great Goddess, so matters may fall out.

She shivered, smiled, and went to the door to summon the scribe.

# IV  THE MOUNTAIN OF GOD

The light of the Star of Bethlehem had gone out: David the son of Jesse slept with his fathers. He had died quietly in the night, eight days after the anointing of his son, and Solomon felt that now indeed he stood alone as king over Israel and Judah.

The immensity of the task appalled him. The well-being, the safety, the comfort of every person lay in his hands; he was the highest judge in their disputes, the chief of battle, the voice of the land to the rest of the world, lawgiver, arbiter, and above all, mediator between his people and God. David had left him a great land; he had conquered the ring of enemies that had circled it so that his son ruled from the pass of Hamath, between Mount Hermon and Mount Lebanon, to the borders of Egypt, and from beyond the Jordan to the shores of the Great Sea. He received tribute from the lords of the cities of Philistia, and from the kings of all the outlying countries except Phoenicia, whose king, Hiram, was his ally and friend. The land had prospered so that the Israelites were as numerous as the sands, and there was peace and plenty from the portion of Dan in the north to the portion of Simeon in the south.

During the last few days before David's death, they had drawn closer together. Now that the first fence had been leveled Solomon sang more of his songs, at first shyly, then with increasing confidence, and David had listened, overjoyed to be thus admitted into the heart of his son, had wept the easy tears of age, and had refrained from making even the smallest criticism of the worst of the verses. By degrees, Solomon had spoken of other things, of his dreams of bringing a lasting peace to the land, of his friendship with Sittar, of his curiosity concerning all of nature and the works of God. And he found that as he spoke his mind received reinforcement from the approval of his father.

On his part, David had tried to bring his son, very gently and obliquely, to see the many facets of government. He had spoken of the need to study the organization of the kingdom, of the need for meeting with and overseeing the officials of the land, and of the deeper requirements of the king: to be accessible but not familiar, to be loved without intimacy, to refrain from tyranny but to hold, nevertheless, the weapon of fear. In this regard, he urged Solomon not to be too lenient with those who had put forward Adonijah, and to let Joab feel his anger.

Above all, he had told Solomon of his ambition to build a great temple to the Lord Yahweh, a dream from which Nathan the prophet had turned him with strong words, saying that the Lord God had never before dwelt in a house but had gone from tent to tent and from dwelling to dwelling from the time he had chosen his people Israel. But, Nathan had added, a son of David's should build a house for the Lord in due time. To that end, David had purchased the threshing floor of Ornan the Jebusite, a wide plain on Mount Moriah, for six hundred shekels of gold. Plans had been drawn up also for the arrangement of the buildings, and David had had men cutting and shaping stone for two years, and had laid by a store of iron clamps and nails, bronze bars, and seasoned logs of cedar purchased from Hiram of Tyre. Solomon swore to his father that the building of the temple would be his first concern.

Then David had said to him, "Keep the charge of the Lord your God by walking in his ways, my son. Keep his statutes, his commandments, his judgments and testimonies as it is written in the Law of Moses, that you may have success in all that you undertake. Thus I may go to the burial cave knowing that the Lord may establish his word to me, saying that if my sons walked before him in truth with all their mind and zeal, there should never fail me a man on the throne of Israel. You are the only one left to me. I look to you, Solomon, my son."

He closed his eyes in weariness, and that night he died.

In the days that followed, Solomon turned more and more often to his God for strength to support him until, as he put it within himself, he had learned to walk. It became his custom to sit upon the rooftop in the evening, after supper, all alone. Not even Zabud would he permit to remain with him, but made the youth rest on the stair below, out of sight, to guard him from interruption. In this hour, lying back upon a low couch, he would watch the stars. Lost among those lambent, mysterious torches he would speak in his heart to Yahweh, who filled the vast dome of heaven, brooding over his people: Such and such a man came with a grievance, have I fully understood the nature of the argument on both sides? The problem of the tribute from Moab which was not paid in full, how shall that be solved? Absalom's old complaint that there were not enough judges in the land to hear all cases, was there place for remedy here? My brother Adonijah: is it possible he may draw some disaffected elements about him to unsettle the kingdom? And what of the thousand details of farms and flocks, vineyards and orchards, taxes and tolls and administration? God, he would pray, give me the strength and intelligence to deal with all of it.

All was still strange to him. He was uncertain of many things and yet too proud to show his uncertainty. If formerly he had disliked criticism, now, in the stiff new garb of royalty, he dreaded it, aware that he might be inadequate to his task.

"O God," he repeated, again and again, "make me worthy."

And anxiously, he waited for a sign, either within himself or in the heavens, the appearance of such an angel as had come to David once, or that uncanny man who wrestled with Jacob, or the bush that burned for Moses. Yet nothing appeared, no voice spoke to him, and in his breast remained the quaking unrest, the bitter self-doubt.

On one such night he ascended the open stair that ran up the outer wall of the palace, with Zabud behind him. He felt particularly restless, for on the morrow he was to go to the high place at Gibeon to make public sacrifice and thus be confirmed in his kingship; it would be, he knew, a long and arduous ceremony.

He stopped a few steps from the top and turned to bid Zabud to remain. The armor-bearer said, "It is a fragrant night, my lord."

Solomon breathed deeply. The scents from the garden rose to him, a joyous exhalation of growth. He said, "Zabud, why do you stay at my heels? Is there no maiden your heart desires, on such a night?"

"There is none for me save my lord the king," Zabud replied in a muffled voice.

"Very well. Sit here, then."

Solomon went up alone as the youth settled himself on a lower step with his back against the outer wall of the palace and a drawn sword across his knees. To come out on the open rooftop was to know liberation from the cage of ceremony that enclosed him all day. The air was very still, the flower-scent and leaf-scent were intoxicating in the glimmering starlight. He leaned both hands on the low parapet, staring at the faint dark outline of the hills to the east. Then he became aware of the fragrance of cinnamon.

There was a presence behind him. He swung round, half in fear. A gray figure bowed low: Abishag, the Shunammite. He knew her as much by her perfume as by the dimly perceived contours of her face and body.

He raised a warning hand before she could address him. He went to the stair and called, "Zabud! Go down further."

"But my lord—" the armor-bearer began.

"Do as I command you," he said firmly.

He saw the dark blot against the white stair waver and move down until it had merged with the shadows. Then he returned to Abishag.

"Why are you here?" he asked, more roughly than he intended because of the sudden hammering of pulses in his throat.

"My lord King David used to come here at night, and at such times I comforted him. It seemed to me that the heart of King Solomon is troubled."

When she addressed him thus, as "King Solomon," he trembled; it was as if she were reminding him of his power.

"If it is so," she continued, "let my lord come and sit beside his servant." She held out her hand.

He took it. It was hot and dry, like one in a fever. He went with her to the couch and they sat side by side. He could feel the warmth come from her body like the warm air that rose from the garden below. He had known women; he was no novice in the delights of love. And Abishag was very beautiful, very desirable; she had stirred him often, before he was anointed king. Now, however, something held him back: perhaps the thought that she was a virgin, perhaps that she had been his father's handmaiden.

"Tell me," he began, then paused. "Did you love my father?" he said.

"I loved him," she answered simply.

For some reason the words woke a feeling of aversion in him. "He was like a father to Abishag, was he not? Do you have no father of your own?"

"I have a father, my lord," she said. "He is a farmer in Shunem. He is dear to me, and yet—was not the king dear to you, my lord? And is not your God dear to you also? As Yahweh is above the king, so was my lord David above my own father for me."

Solomon said gloomily, "Did my father ever call on his God to no purpose?"

"No one calls on Yahweh in vain," she said, a note of surprise in her voice.

"And if there is no answer? No—sign?"

"The time of God is not the time of man. He will answer in his own time."

"No wonder David held Abishag in such esteem. She has an answer for everything."

There was silence for a moment. Then, in a small voice, she said, "Does the king wish his servant to depart?"

"No. Do not go."

It burst from him against his will, for at that moment he wished that she had never come, that she had left him in peace with his thoughts.

"Do I find no favor with my lord?" she asked, almost in a sob.

He took her hand again in both of his. "Abishag is very lovely," he replied. Her hand stirred, as if he held her heart between his palms. The night was like a warm, sweet-smelling tent enclosing them secretly. Solomon embraced her and drew her down among the cushions.

"Did you come to comfort the king?" he whispered, into the tumbled mass of her hair. "I am not he. I am only a man."

On the high place at Gibeon, among the foothills of the mountains of Ephraim, stood the tent of meeting which Moses had made in the desert, for a House of the Lord. It was made from eleven curtains of black goats' hair, joined together with bronze clasps and protected by a covering of rams' skins. Within it was the dwelling of Yahweh, the secret place made of curtains of fine linen dyed violet, purple and scarlet, and embroidered with cherubim. A table of acacia wood overlaid with gold stood before it, bearing the vessels for libation and the bread of the Presence. Only the Ark, the worn, ancient wooden chest containing the decrees which Yahweh gave to Moses, was not there, for it rested in a tent in Jerusalem where David had brought it out of the hands of the Philistines. Before the tent of meeting was an altar of bronze, and here the sacrifices for all Israel were made to God.

Below the mountain of Gibeon was a village, where the priests might live when their turn came to minister to the altar. This had been made a green and pleasant place. But in the mountain of God, the wind blew through stunted and gnarled trees, the ground was parched and bare, and the air was filled with gray loneliness and with awe. Not even the ranks of people, the brilliant colors of the garments of captains and chieftains who crowded the hilltop and all the slopes, could disturb this air; nor could the intense heat of the altar, the piles of glowing ash, the smoke of burnt offerings remove the chill of desolation.

It struck Solomon to the heart, for he felt that God had removed from him. He was unclean; he had lain with a woman on the night before this holy ceremony. He stood before the altar with the sweat pouring down his face, watching with glazed eyes the steady work of butchering, the busy priests raking out cinders and refueling the fire, dismembering the carcasses and giving to each of the people the prescribed share. Hundreds of smaller fires had been kindled, and everywhere men were cooking their portions. The sweetish smell of blood was in Solomon's nostrils, and the odor of roasting meat had lost its savor and only sickened him.

All that day he stood, and save for a little wine and a mouthful of meat from the first sacrifice, he ate nothing, for he could not force himself to swallow. His very skin seemed to be burning, his eyes and mouth were dry. Toward evening, he began to feel insubstantial, as if his whole being had been withered away to the subtlest essences; he no longer felt the weight of his body, his knees ceased to shake, he became light as a spirit.

As the sun was setting, Zadok the priest came to him, wiping his hands upon a napkin. His vestments were stained with blood and grease, and he looked ready to drop with weariness.

"Will my lord the king go down to the tent that has been prepared for him?" he asked.

"No," said Solomon, in a voice that was strange to his own ears. "Let all depart. I will remain here alone."

"But, my lord, you must rest—"

"Must?" Solomon's eyes, gleaming with an unearthly light, turned upon the priest so that Zadok shrank back. "Go, I say. As for me, I must do only as God commands."

Zadok backed away. Soon the long lines of men filed down the mountain singing; the priests followed—all but those whose duty it was to guard the tabernacle. The moon, thin and curved like an Egyptian sword, rose among mists. A mountain wind, fresh and cold, swept the air clean and rattled the leather coverings of the tent of meeting.

Solomon wrapped himself in his cloak and walked away from the altar. Behind the tabernacle, on the hillside, was a grove of oaks, twisted and wind-blown, clutching the stony ground with frantic roots. Here he came and rested against a tree trunk.

That he had lain with a woman was, he now saw, not the true source of his sense of impurity. He had looked into Abishag's face this morning when, robed and crowned, he had left the palace to go to Gibeon. She had been radiant with love. But although he had desired her to solace his loneliness, he had not loved her; he did not love her now. He had taken her virginity as carelessly as a shepherd picks a meadow flower to tuck behind his ear. He could return her nothing. He had looked at her coldly, not returning her smile, and before his distant face pain had swept into her eyes. She had shrunk back, effacing herself as she had always done. It was as if a shadow had fallen over her, consigning her to darkness.

Was this to be his reign, ill-omened as it had begun? He who wished for peace had ascended the throne in strife with his brother. He who wished for all men to love one another had dealt this wound to Abishag.

He sank down, burdened as much by guilt as by fatigue. It came to him with horror that he knew this grove: it was here that the seven of the House of Saul had been hanged. That had happened in the reign of his father, when there had been a famine in the land. The voice of the Lord, speaking through the uncompromising mouth of the prophet Nathan, had said that this was a punishment for the misdeeds of King Saul, who had slain some of the men of Gibeon. In expiation, seven men of the seed of Saul had been given to the Gibeonites as a blood payment; two were the sons of Rizpah, Saul's consort, and five were the sons of Merab the daughter of Saul. All had been brought to this grove on the mountain of the Lord, and hanged upon these trees in the first days of the barley harvest.

The ancient boughs creaked and swayed as if their burdens still weighed heavily upon them. In the night wind he heard the wild cries of Rizpah, who for a whole month had remained with the bodies of her sons, driving away the ravens and vultures. Madness and pain, sorrow and death—the grove was charged with them. He felt them rush into him and through him, like barbed arrows through his frail and ghostly flesh.

"My God!" he cried aloud, "do not close your ears to your servant."

Darkness rose before his eyes, and he sank down into it as if toward Sheol, the pit of emptiness. Then a pale light grew in the grove, and he saw that the trees had grown enormous and transparent; the light shone from their very trunks, as if the core of each were burning.

Then he thought that a voice, majestic beyond endurance, bodiless and breathless, without tone or resonance, and yet shaking him to the soul, said, "Solomon."

"Lord," he said, "I am here."

And he thought that the voice said, "Why does not Solomon my servant sacrifice before me?"

"My God," said Solomon, "I am full of evil. But I have sacrificed a thousand burnt offerings this day on the altar of the Lord."

"What are burnt offerings to me?" said the voice. "Each man must sacrifice what is most dear to him, to receive from me his desire. Ask what I shall give you."

"Lord, you have shown great loving-kindness to David my father, and have made me king in his stead," said Solomon. "Now, O God, let your promise to David my father be established, for you have made me king over a people as numerous as the dust of the earth. Let me be king indeed."

"Be king, first, over yourself," said the voice.

Solomon covered his face with his hands. "Give me wisdom and knowledge," he said, "that I may know how to go out and come in before your people. Lord, give your servant an attentive mind to judge your people in righteousness and to discern between good and evil. And I will set upon the altar of Yahweh my own self, devoting myself to follow the wishes of my God and to rule over Israel."

The voice said, so that the words were like the rolling of thunder, "Because you have asked this thing and have not asked for yourself long life nor riches nor the lives of your enemies, behold I have done according to your word: I have given you a wise and discerning mind so that there has been none like you before you, and none like you shall arise after you. I have also given you what you did not ask: both riches and honor, so that all your days there shall not be any like you among the kings. If you walk in my ways so that you keep my statutes and my commandments then I will prolong your days."

With that, the Presence left him; he felt it move from the grove as the light faded and the darkness returned.

He knew that he was dreaming, but he saw himself asleep under the hand of the Lord, and leaving his body he ascended above the trees, high above the land that was spread out below him with all its houses, all its sheepfolds, all its vineyards and orchards and fields of grain, its mountain gorges and wildernesses and rivers. His shadow fell over all of it, from Dan to Beersheba.

He awoke, and full of joy, made his way back to the tent of meeting.

# part two

# 1
THE SHUNAMMITE

During the first years of Solomon's reign, the busiest man in all Israel was Jehoshaphat the son of Ahilud, the king's recorder. All day and far into the night he labored with his ten secretaries, using great bundles of reed pens and mountains of sheepskin to set down all that was accomplished by the king. He had little leisure for reflection, yet now and then when he took exercise by walking with his hands behind his back, his beard wagging, between the two rows of men scratching over their records, he would think: God has indeed blessed our lord King Solomon with wisdom and fervor so that the wish of Benaiah has come to pass, and his throne is truly greater than the throne of his father, King David.

Never before had Israel known such prosperity nor so many rapid changes in so short a time. Solomon was everywhere, indefatigable and energetic, bursting with ideas, secure in his covenant with Yahweh. Ever since that night in the grove of Gibeon his heart had been uplifted; it was as if with every moment of furious activity he shouted his thanks to God. His dream had been written and was known to the whole land, and it was clear to everyone that his acts and decisions could only be inspired by divine power. Wherever he appeared—in his court at judgment, driving out in his chariot, traveling to one or another part of the kingdom, walking through farms or fields, or inspecting the building of new fortresses and roads—shining faces and blessings greeted him.

He had begun by strengthening trade relations with his neighbors. His embassies went to Egypt and to Aram and to the lands beyond, and he brought from those countries craftsmen who were skilled in metalwork, in weaving, in pottery and in carpentry, to teach their arts to Israel. To further tighten the bonds abroad he made two advantageous marriages: with Mahalath, a noblewoman of Sidon and kin to King Hiram of Tyre; and with Tuosri, one of the daughters of Psusennes, Pharaoh of Egypt. These two women he established in houses of their own in the city until he might build a palace to accommodate them.

His love for horses brought him to the import of steeds from Egypt, where his father-in-law gave him excellent prices, and he began to build up the core of what was later to become an immense force of cavalry and chariots, not only for the defense of the land but for speed of communication. Roads, too, were widened so that chariots could pass everywhere, and he built fortified cities and store-cities in which companies of charioteers and horsemen were stationed. At Megiddo he constructed enormous stables to accommodate five hundred horses and over a hundred chariots, with barracks for the great force of men required to care for them.

Very soon, he was importing horses from Cilicia as well as Egypt, and selling them to the Hittites and Aramaeans. Iron and copper also he traded, for his land was rich in both, and at Ezion-geber, in the distant south, he established a mine and smelter which was the wonder of the world. There, too, on the shores of the Red Sea he commenced the construction of a seaport from which he planned to send ships to trade with the southern lands in ivory and sandalwood, gold, precious stones, and feathers. From King Hiram he secured seamen to act as the leaders of his crews and to train up Israelite sailors.

To deal with the volume of trade, he established new officials and reorganized the administration of the land, setting up twelve governors to oversee all parts of the country, making them responsible to a single officer and to himself. Each of the twelve also took it in turn to provide provisions for the king's household. He appointed garrison commanders, and set a severe old man, Azariah the son of Nathan, over them. Benaiah the son of Jehoiada he made captain of his entire army in place of Joab, against whom he took no other action, since the son of Zeruiah was advanced in years and had served his father faithfully for so long a time.

In Jerusalem itself he wrought affectionately and tirelessly, building new houses, bringing in precious metals and carved work, increasing the wealth of the men of his city until it was said that silver and gold were as common as stone, and cedar as plentiful as the sycamores of the lowlands.

In all this industry he had many counselors to advise him, but the chief and dearest of them was Abishag the Shunammite. When he had made his peace with God and with himself, he had at the same time made his peace with her.

He had gone to her soon after the day of sacrifice, bringing her up to the high chamber which he now made his library and private study, and had said, "As God lives, Abishag, I will not put you forth from me. But I will not make you my wife, for I do not love you. Nor will I shame you further by making you my consort. Remain here, however, and be the king's friend."

She had said submissively, "Be it as my lord wills."

But the dark look of pain had not left her face. She had gone about the house like a shadow, speaking seldom, always gentle and winsome but hardly more than a wraith. So, at last, he had commanded her to come to the rooftop, where he still sat for one hour each day after the evening meal to be undisturbed, to rest, and to think. At these times, he sat with Abishag and they conversed, and he found that he could unburden his heart to her as to no one else. He came to talk of all his plans—for speaking aloud was to confirm and clarify them in his mind—and by degrees he saw that she was wise in her own right, quick to perceive weaknesses, shrewd to point out the path through obstacles, and inclined always toward what might be best for the whole land. He came to rely on her more and more, and as their intimacy increased, the cloud lifted from her, the lines of sorrow were smoothed away from her face, and there grew up between them another sort of love: on Solomon's part the deep affection of a brother for a sister, and on Abishag's, contentment that she should be admitted to his confidence and so, at least, be near him, retain a part of him that was hers alone.

It was she who raised the vexing question of Joab.

They were upon the rooftop, Solomon sitting on the low parapet, and Abishag on the divan, which she had drawn close to him. She sat cross-legged with a small lute on her lap and idly plucked the strings. The air above was darkening, and in its melting depths, the first star shone, but over the hills beyond Hinnom bars of gray and pink striped a sky of liquid gold. Solomon was looking toward the northeast, where the view had already changed. Where once the threshing floor of Ornan the Jebusite had lain, with its open barns and its altar to the goddess Khepa, now stood lofty walls of stone gilded by the sunset, roofs of cedar, great pillars and soaring towers. A little way below were the geometric shapes of scaffolding overlying the irregular lines of unfinished buildings.

"I never tire of looking upon it," he said.

Abishag smiled. "My lord is like a father watching his first-born. Full of pride . . ."

He glanced at her. "I hear and understand. Abishag has never spared me, but speaks as the voice of my conscience. You mean that I must beware lest I admire my own ability rather than the perfection of the House of God."

He swung round, clasping his hands about one knee. Four years had changed him little to the eye: he was as sparely built as ever, graceful and quick, a little heavier in the chest and shoulders but still with the lithe alertness of a dancer. Only, now, he wore his nobility more easily; the mantle of kingship lay with an accustomed lightness on his body. He had developed an inward strength, bracing to meet each new burden until he could bear it unflinchingly. He was like a soldier to whom first the heaviness of spear, shield and sword are intolerable, but who learns to carry them like a second self until he may vault walls without considering their weight.

He said, "I recognize my pride, Abishag. But the Temple and the palaces are not mine, but Israel's. I am the servant of Yahweh and of his people." He looked again over his shoulder at the distant buildings. "I love them, those walls and roofs and towers, for they are the symbol of Israel's greatness, the sign shown to the whole world of the Lord's covenant with my father, David, when he said, 'I will appoint a place for my people Israel, and will plant them, that they may dwell in their own place. Your house and your kingdom shall be confirmed before me forever, and for all time your throne shall be established.'"

His face shone as he said this, his teeth gleaming in a smile within his beard. "A great people," he repeated, "for all time," looking as he did so at the high vault of heaven.

Abishag struck a note or two, thin and melodious, and then said, "What God has promised he will accomplish. But he will not do all for Solomon. You must lift up your own hand, to make secure the kingdom."

"Yes."

"If rats come to gnaw the house, the husbandman must destroy them. He cannot wait for them to die of old age, in the fullness of time."

He brought his attention back to her. "What is this riddle?" he said.

She lifted her gaze from the strings of the lute, peering soberly at him through the gathering gloaming. "Surely my lord knows that the son of Zeruiah has returned to Jerusalem?"

"Ah . . . so it is Joab."

"When my lord asked, last month, if he should allow the son of Zeruiah to live in the city again, I advised against it."

"I cannot bar Joab from the Dedication of the Temple. For all his wrongdoing, he served my father with love and faithfulness. He stood beside him through the years of danger and privation, through his outlawry and his service among the Philistines, through the black years and the hard establishment of his throne. Whatever Joab did —and there is murder on his hands—he did with my father's good in mind."

"And afterward, Adonijah's good," she commented wryly.

"Yes. But I have forbidden him to see my face for four years. It is long enough, and he is an old man."

"Not too old for intrigue."

The king rose abruptly, and stood looking down at her. He said, "Abishag is oftener inclined to mercy and kindness than am I. It is clear to me that she is not speaking lightly. What is it, then?"

She laid by the lute and sat erect. "My lord, I have heard that Joab means to bring a petition to the king tomorrow. He will ask that Solomon make him a commander of the host once more."

Solomon first frowned, then shrugged. "He is a stiff-necked man. How many times was he set aside by my father, and yet always returned? Now he thinks to do the same with me. But I will not remove Benaiah for him nor any other man."

"My lord heard me wrong. I did not say he wishes to become captain of the host, but *a* commander. He will petition the king to let him return his sword to the service of Israel, for he has said, 'I am like an old war horse, unfit for anything save battle. I cannot graze nor pull a plow; I am too tough to be eaten, even by the desert men.'"

Solomon burst into laughter. "As God lives, he does not lack for stoutness of heart. Well, then? Why should I deny him?"

"His petition is that he be made commander of the king's body-guard."

The king clasped his hands behind his back, pondering. "Is this too much for him to ask? It may be he wishes to make his peace with me for once and all. How better can he show it than in a post of honor?"

"Not so." She was too perturbed to keep from directly contradicting him. She stood up and set her hand on his arm. "My lord," she said, "consider."

"What troubles Abishag?" he asked, gently.

"Joab is an Ishmaelite. He is like the Bedouins, he never forgets a grievance. Nor does he willingly yield up what he has set his hand to. Does Solomon know that when he returned to the city he went at once to call upon Adonijah?"

"I have heard that."

"And that they have been closeted together several times since then? My lord, remember Abner—he who was formerly captain of Saul's host. He slew Asahel, the brother of Joab, and for this Joab never forgave him, but murdered him afterwards in cold blood, when the man thought all was over between them. The son of Zeruiah is tenacious; he is like a serpent that lies low in the dust and bites the heel that treads on him."

She gripped his sleeve tightly in her anxiety. "Where better can he conceal himself than in the king's own chamber? How can he come closer to the king than as commander of his bodyguard? Well does he know that he will never twist Solomon to suit his purposes. It is Adonijah who is his friend and companion. Why should the king think that Joab has given up his hope to oust Solomon and seat Adonijah upon the throne, to be revenged upon Benaiah who was made captain of the host in his place, and to make himself a power in the land once more?"

Solomon touched her lightly on the cheek. "These are all guesses," he said.

"But, my lord—"

"Hush! Let me think."

She released him, and he turned away, setting one foot on the parapet and staring out toward the now darkened pile of the Temple and the unfinished palaces upon Mount Moriah. His imagination pierced the gloom, seeing clearly the stately courses of stone and squared timbers, the carved doors and doorposts, the golden ornaments. The palace, the house of women, the judgment hall, the throne room—all these lacked some years of being finished. But the Temple was nearly done; another four or five weeks would suffice for the finishing touches, the last bits of gold leaf, the last polishings and paintings. As he had told Abishag, the Temple had become the symbol of his reign, but he had not said aloud what she had so clearly fathomed in any case: that it was the living shape of his achievements.

And he thought, If there were within it a rotten beam, would I not replace it?

If Abishag was right, and Joab meant him evil, it would be the height of folly to give him opportunity. If his intentions were good it would be wrong to make an enemy of him. Still, he thought, if he is to come before me again he must learn humility, he must know that his wish bends to the king's will.

"Well," he said, "it may be you are right, although some might think it no more than a woman's fancy. I will make Joab commander of the garrison at Tamar, my new city on the border, and governor of the city as well."

"Then you will deny his petition?"

"I will not wait for that. I will send my command to him early tomorrow. Thus it will seem I desire to honor him without knowing of his petition. Also, on the day of the dedication of the Temple, I will put him at my own side. Thus his ambition should be satisfied. Does this please Abishag?"

"My lord," she said, softly, "it has nothing to do with pleasing or not pleasing me. It is the safety of Solomon that concerns me, for—" Her voice faltered, and she went on, "For the sake of Israel."

"I know it well, my sister," he replied affectionately. "In four days more my Temple will be dedicated to Yahweh. Until that is over, not even the son of Zeruiah has the power to distress me."

He turned from her and went to the stair.

*My sister!* she thought, looking after him. And her longing fretted her like a knife dulled with long use.

Joab loved to break his fast among soldiers. In the long common room with its rough benches and earth floor he felt most at home; dipping into the bowl of curds and breaking chunks of barley bread with the guardsmen, he was more at his ease than he ever was in palaces or great houses. All knew him, some of the veterans had served under him, and they treated him with the respectful familiarity that was the due of a seasoned old officer.

The low-ceilinged room was full of noise, pungent with the smell of many men squeezed together. Across the table from Joab a brawny file-leader was telling a soldier's tale hallowed by antiquity, a story which had never varied in a thousand years, well known to every man who ever served in an army, and beloved as the face of a dear friend:

". . . so I go with her to her house. May I be a dog's head if it was not a palace! She said to me, 'Sit down and wait, drink wine,

I will be with you in a moment.' I did so, and in a little while she comes back dressed only in a wisp of something you could see right through . . ."

"Uzzi, you are the greatest liar in Jerusalem."

"May I wither where I sit if it is not true! Men! She was as beautiful as the day—a body like new milk—breasts like pomegranates—"

Joab chuckled, and said, "Tell us, Uzzi, did you eat her or make love to her?"

They roared at that, as if he had said the funniest thing in the world, although the jest, too, was traditional. He sat back on the bench, grinning and licking curds from his fingers, and as he did so a man pushed his way through the crowded room and touched him on the back.

"What is it?" Joab asked, over his shoulder.

"For the son of Zeruiah, a message from our lord King Solomon."

Joab took the waxed tablets, touched them perfunctorily to his forehead, and sat for a moment holding them in his hand. Then he picked up his staff and rose. "I will hear the rest of Uzzi's tale tomorrow," he said. "Surely he will not have finished it by then."

Still smiling, he made his way into the sunny courtyard where groups of men, off duty, were sitting scratching themselves or polishing armor. He found a quiet spot in an angle of the wall, and breaking the thread, opened the tablets.

As he read the king's word the blood rushed to his head. The sunlight was blotted out by a red haze, and fury strangled him so that he gasped for breath. Catching himself, he read the message through again to see if, by chance, he had overlooked something, some phrase or words that might tell him he had misunderstood it: ". . . to the command of my new city of Tamar . . . over all the horsemen and chariots . . . and to be governor . . ."

He clapped the tablets together and for a moment almost flung them to the ground. His face burned and he was deprived of coherent thought, so that disconnected words raced through his mind—*insulted, cast out, a mockery*—then he mastered himself. He shook off weakness and rage, becoming icily calm as was his way. He walked to the gates, smiling and nodding to the men he passed and returning their greetings. In the street his chariot stood, his armor-bearer, Gareb the Ithrite, dozing in it with his feet sprawled outside. Joab struck him across the soles with the end of his staff, and the man awoke.

"Up," said Joab, "and drive me to the field in Hinnom where Adonijah is practicing with the bow."

He mounted into the chariot, gripping the rim with both hands. Gareb stood before him, his legs braced wide apart, yawning as he guided the horses without effort.

The chariot lurched under Joab's feet, and he bent his knees to take up the shock of ruts and stones beneath the wheels. He was too old to drive himself any longer, to hold the reins and balance himself against the swaying of the car. He looked down at his hands, deeply wrinkled, with raised veins like dark cords lying upon the sunburned skin, and crisp white hairs growing thickly on his knuckles. Too old . . . easily shamed, easily cast aside, shuffled off to a border station to end his days like a toothless dog in the sands of the desert.

The stiffness of age was upon him. His knees would not even respond any longer to the bouncing of the chariot. The quick responses of youth were long gone, the ability to strike, to kill, to act without deliberation and to save himself on the impulse of the moment, by instinct as it were. Now all that was left him was slow thought that allowed him to be outmaneuvered; where once he had dashed on horseback, now he plodded like a foot soldier in the dust. Even his old companions were gone, even his king whom he had loved in his own way with a deep, burning love. All that was left to him were the dry rinds of hate, the leavings of the dish, thrown to him by Solomon.

"That dead dog, may Yahweh consume him with his throne," he muttered, grinding his teeth.

"My lord?" Gareb shouted.

"Nothing, fool. Drive on."

They came down into the vale of Hinnom. At the foot of the hills, under the shadow of the walls of the city, there was a wide, flat place planted with a double row of oak trees. Stakes had been set at either end some fifty paces apart, with shields hanging from them. As Gareb brought the chariot to a halt, there was a burst of applause from the group of men who stood watching the archery.

Adonijah had just shot, and was drawing his bow to shoot again. His eyes flicked toward Joab, then away; he stood firm as a rock, the muscles of his arms swelling against the tension of the bow. The string sounded a harp note. Jehiel, his armor-bearer, who stood beside him holding his quiver, shouted, "In the boss! Five!"

Joab strode up to the prince. "The son of Haggith plays well with toys," he growled.

"Toys?" Adonijah chuckled. "I never thought to hear the captain

of the host sneer at weapons. Is there another archer in the land
who can hit the boss five times running?"

"Captain—?" Joab clenched his teeth. "Come apart with me a little way."

Adonijah tossed his bow to Jehiel. Nebat the Ephraimite stood
nearby with his hands behind his back, and Joab beckoned to him
also. He led the two younger men aside and sat down in the shade.

"I have been dismissed," he said. "He is tossing me the captaincy
of a city in the desert, as my bone."

Adonijah said, "He has denied your petition? He is shrewder than
we thought, not to let you come near his person."

"Shrewder than we think indeed," said Joab coldly, "seeing that
I have not yet handed in my petition. He has forestalled me. Here
is his letter; see, he writes that it rejoices his heart to hear that I
have returned to Jerusalem, that he freely forgives me all my past
errors, and that to show his love for me it pleases him to promote
me to the command of his new city, Tamar . . . and so on."

He looked up at the small, scalloped leaves over his head. "Pro-
moted," he said, grimly. "Is he so wise as they say? Could he have
foreseen my move? Or has word somehow come to him of my intentions? None knew save you two."

"What is said among three is soon known by ten," said Nebat. "A
servant may have overheard, told it to another, and so it got to the
ears of the king's gazelle, who knows all. This is her doing, I will
swear it."

"Of whom does Nebat speak?" asked Joab.

"I had forgotten that the son of Zeruiah has not yet learned all
the news. Of Abishag the Shunammite."

"Yes. He calls her sister," Adonijah said. "By my hand, I would
she were sister to me."

"He has not wed her?" said Joab. "He keeps her by him?"

"As if she were his consort, yet he never goes in to her. He has
not taken her to wife, but he holds her in high esteem and all the
palace knows he will do nothing save by her advice. She has edged
out Nathan, Benaiah, his counselors, even his mother."

"Even Bathsheba? Now this is news to me," said Joab, thoughtfully. He glanced up at Adonijah from under his thick eyelids. "And
is Abishag still fair to look upon? I remember her as not much more
than a child, slight, and dark."

"She is no child. She is beautiful," Adonijah said, cracking his
knuckles. "If I yet come to the throne I wish she may be my chief

counselor. It may be I will have something to teach her that she does not know."

The old man sat silent for a long time so that it almost seemed he had forgotten their presence. Then he lifted his head. He was smiling, a cold and lipless smile like that of a lizard.

"Adonijah," he said, "come, put away your bow and bathe and dress yourself. We are going to visit an old and dear enemy of mine, who nevertheless may receive me with joy."

Bathsheba had just finished administering a long and complicated scolding to the steward Ahishar, when the son of Haggith and the son of Zeruiah were announced to her. Formerly, she had enjoyed these scenes, asserting her perfect domination over the house, lashing with her tongue the incompetent and thoughtless among her servants, but now they merely depressed her and served to emphasize that she herself was little more than a kind of housekeeper, no longer the best beloved wife of the king, but the mother of a king who paid her scant attention. It was hard for her to recognize her own son these days. He had grown regal, and hence distant. He still greeted her dutifully and kindly, but she felt herself pushed to the periphery of his life. She was no longer courted or visited by petitioners, and often she had nothing whatever to do but sit alone, her back as straight as ever but her hands idle. In consequence, even the visit of Joab and Adonijah was a welcome relief, and she told the servant to admit them.

She received them in the garden, seated on a bench under a great fig tree heavy with purple fruit. She did not rise, but greeted them with a severe inclination of the head. Joab bowed deeply, and after a moment's hesitation, Adonijah did likewise.

"Well, son of Zeruiah," she said, ignoring the prince, "is your coming friendly?"

"Lady, it is friendly," said Joab. "Since I have returned to Jerusalem, I thought well to make obeisance to you, for the sake of old memories. For I do not forget quickly, neither enemies nor friends, and King David was my lord and companion for many years."

Her expression did not change, only at the name her eyes softened. "For the sake of that memory, then, be welcome," she said.

She indicated that they should sit down upon the ground. Adonijah did so, but Joab remained standing, leaning upon his olivewood staff.

"Yes," he said, shaking his head mournfully, "to forget is in the nature of men. I have returned and found myself dimmed to a shadow in the minds of those who called themselves my friends. Only our lord Solomon, of whose wisdom all speak, deserves his reputation. Yes, putting aside the wrongs I did him he gave me, out of his bounty, the post of governor over the city of Tamar. Where I might least have looked for it, he has remembered his servant, Joab."

Watching her closely, he saw her lips tighten and he smiled within himself. He went on, "Joyful is it to a mother's heart when her son ascends the throne, and she herself is raised up to his right hand to be the adviser and overseer of a king."

At this, words were forced out of her in a creaking voice. "Such a mother is fortunate. Let the son of Zeruiah show me such a one that I may behold her with envy."

He opened his eyes wide. "What do I hear?" he said.

"Nothing that is not common knowledge. Let Joab not stare; I am no more than an outcast. I no longer have the ear of my son. My place has been taken by another." Now that she had begun to speak of it, she found pleasure in unburdening herself of bitterness. "Are we not warned to beware of an ungrateful son? He comes and speaks fairly to me with a soft voice, but puts me away from his counsels and listens instead to Abishag. Shameful is it before all his advisers, but the greatest shame is that on his mother's head."

"Abishag?" said Joab, as if the name were surprising to him. "The Shunammite? Why, here is a wonder! As God sees me, it is beyond belief. For it was concerning Abishag that we wished to speak with you."

Her face grew suspicious again. "With me?"

"Let Adonijah tell you. For it was he who prayed me to bring him to you, fearing that if he came alone you might refuse to hear him."

Adonijah nodded, scratching at the roots of his coarse beard. "The lady Bathsheba must believe me," he said, "when I tell her that whatever was, is past. She has been cold to me all this while, remembering that I tried to proclaim myself king—although in truth I did no more than claim what was mine. For does not the Law say that a man must give the right of the first-born to the first-born, and if he be the son of a slighted wife nevertheless he must have two-thirds of all that his father owns? Such is the Law! And my mother, Haggith, on whose memory be peace—"

Joab seemed to totter; his staff slipped from the ground as if by accident and struck Adonijah in the chest. "Forgive me," he said, recovering himself, and as he did so he darted a fell glance at the prince.

Adonijah caught himself, stammered once or twice, and then went on, "No matter. I relinquish it all. Let the past be buried between us. Now I have been living quietly, doing nothing to draw attention to myself, and I will go on this way. There is little I ask. But one thing I wish for, one thing I desire for my happiness—a small thing —the maiden Abishag."

Bathsheba stared at him. He continued quickly, "Our lord Solomon will not listen to me, for he still fears I have designs on the kingdom. But if you make a request of him, surely he will not refuse you. Suggest, I pray you, to the king that he give me the Shunammite as a wife."

Astonishment held Bathsheba motionless. In the silence, Joab interposed smoothly, "See, lady, how pat this jumps with your own desire. For at one stroke, Bathsheba may make an ally and friend of the son of Haggith, and remove from between her son and herself the wall that holds them apart."

"I see," Bathsheba said, "that you have concocted this between you for your own purposes."

"It rejoices me," Joab said, in a gentle tone, "to be the means of bringing mother and son together, and two lovers as well. Blessed is the hand that joins those who love one another! If there is any other purpose in my heart, God sees it and will punish me."

"No doubt." She rose up, haughty and straight. "Nevertheless, I will help you. I will ask this of the king. But not now."

"Why not?" Adonijah said, with a frown. "If Bathsheba fears duplicity, I swear to her—"

"I fear nothing. Inasmuch as my son is occupied with preparing for the dedication of the Temple, I judge the time unripe. After the Feast of Booths, his mind will be full of happiness as a man's is after a great ambition is satisfied. That will be the readiest time to secure his consent."

They bowed to her. Joab took her hand and placed it against his forehead. "As God lives," he said, "the lady Bathsheba knows that I am her friend, now and forever."

"I am content," Bathsheba said, sourly. "God forbid I should stand between two lovers."

They looked at each other, smiling a trifle, and between them was the perfect understanding of mutual dislike.

The olive harvest was in, and the golden oil stored away; the vines had been stripped and the mountains of grapes pressed into wine. The grain had been cut with flint-edged sickles, or by the richer farmers, with new iron sickles, and threshed out on stone floors. And now, on the fifteenth day of the month of Ethanim, Jerusalem resembled a city under siege. Every house bulged with visiting friends or relatives; every inch of ground outside the walls was covered either with goatskin tents or with little arbors made of green branches. From every part of the land the people of Israel trooped —all who could possibly come—for the festival of the in-gathering, for this new year would begin with the dedication of the House of the Lord built by King Solomon, and all who were there would not only see wonders but would feast as the king's guests.

Solomon rose early and looked out upon the perfect day. It was as if he stood within a vast hive: the hum of the multitude rose to the palace windows. He looked toward his Temple, shining and beautiful, and said within himself, "Lord, keep me from pride on this day, save pride in your love."

Zabud greeted him with a happy smile, threw a robe over his shoulders and led him to the bath. He washed, and oiled himself, and the armor-bearer combed his hair. For this day, he chose to dress himself simply in a plain white tunic and kirtle to show himself the humblest of God's servants; it was enough that he would wear the crown.

The palace was full of guests, like the town. Two of Solomon's uncles with their families had come up from Judah, and there were envoys from Egypt, Tyre, and Aram, who had to be housed. Bath-sheba had, for once, put aside her fretting, for she had more than enough work to do and the servants flew about under her direction like leaves before the wind. When Solomon came down to the common room she had been up for hours, bustling about.

She looked at him, and put her hands to her throat, her breath catching in a sob. He was so tall and comely, so like a king! And from his proud face, the eyes of her beloved looked forth, the large, warm, quick eyes of David that saw everything and held compassion for all.

She went to him and put her hands on his shoulders, gazing up at him wistfully. "My son," she said. She wanted to tell him how much she loved him on this day of all days when he would show to the world the greatness of his people. But instead, she said, "Why did you choose to wear white? Is this seemly for the king? And before the eyes of the foreign envoys—"

He took her face between his hands. "My mother has never ceased to think of me as her babe," he said, laughing. "Whatever the king wears is seemly."

"Now you mock me," she said, petulantly.

"No, no. Only let me wear what I will. Did the Lord not say to Moses, 'When you have a king, let him stand in awe of the Lord, for he is not more exempt than the rest from the Law.' It is to show forth that the king of Israel is no more than a man that I wear these clothes."

He looked at her, but saw only annoyance and incomprehension in her face. He sighed, and said, "I will wear a golden collar and a golden belt. These, with the crown, will make me look princely enough. Does this please my mother?"

He turned from her, then, for Benaiah had come with Joel the son of Abner, who had been given the post of commander of the bodyguard, and who brought with him the picked men for the day. Solomon had diminished this force from a thousand to six hundred men, and to emphasize that their use was decorative and peaceful, had given them gilded helmets and had covered the faces of their shields with plates of pure gold. The fifty who were to walk before and behind him on this day were ranked in the courtyard, and their shields all together made a dazzling light.

When he had greeted his two captains, and sent the guardsmen to wait outside the gates, the king then had leisure to drink a single glass of wine. He would eat nothing until the sacrifices were made. He embraced the foreign envoys, giving each of them rich presents of fine robes to wear for the festival. Then Zabud brought him the crown and a collar and belt, as he had promised Bathsheba, and when he was arrayed he went forth into the street.

David had brought the Ark to a tent in Jerusalem, pitched on an earthen platform at the highest point of the city. Here, Zadok the high priest waited, and with him were the elders of the council, the chiefs of the tribes in gorgeously striped and tasseled cloaks, the twelve governors of the land, and Solomon's brothers, the princes, including Adonijah, whose jewels made a burden that would have bent a slighter man double. Joab, also, was there, and Solomon took him by the hand and said, "You shall walk at my right side to show all men that the king has utterly forgiven you."

Joab bowed low, and replied with an expression of humility and affection, "My lord the king is too generous." His gaze met that of Benaiah, who stood behind Solomon, and he said, "Yet it might be fitter if I were to walk behind the captain of the host seeing that I am once again a soldier, and that I once did him a wrong."

The eyes of the son of Jehoiada were clear and honest. He smiled at Joab, and said, "Not so. Whatever quarrel lay between us is past. For myself, I feel only joy that our lord the king has restored the son of Zeruiah to his favor. The post of honor beside the king should be his."

Solomon said, "Come. Let Joab delay no longer."

"Well, I will walk where our lord the king commands—in this as in all other matters," said Joab.

The rams' horns sounded. Zadok faced the tent. Out of it came four priests bearing on their shoulders the staves that held the Ark. In the sun, the worn and ancient wood glistened as if with a mellow light of its own. Within it were the stone tablets which Moses had engraved with the words of the Law, and at the sight of this most holy of objects, all who were there involuntarily covered their faces.

Zadok held up his arms. He was noble to behold. On his breast gleamed the ephod of gold, violet, purple and scarlet, bearing two onyx stones on which were cut the names of the twelve tribes, and above this hung an oracle pouch of linen on which were twelve precious stones bearing the same names. About his head was a diadem of gold on which was written, 'Sacred to the Lord,' and on the hem of his robe were tiny golden bells that tinkled as he moved. "Behold, Israel," he cried. "The Ark of the Covenant between you and the Lord your God."

"Blessed be his name forever," said Solomon.

He went forth, then, with all the princes and chieftains around him, set as it were in the flashing golden shields of the bodyguard, and behind him came Zadok and the Ark. After the Ark came other priests bearing the various panels and sections of the tent of meeting, which had been taken from the high place at Gibeon, together with its table and lampstand and serving implements, all to be brought now to the Temple.

The hill called Moriah lay to the northeast of the city, separated from it by a shallow valley. It was not very high, but covered almost as much ground as David's city, and near its top was the flat space which had once been a threshing floor, with the rough stone altar on which the first fruits had been offered to Khepa by the Jebusites. Now, the entire hill was covered with the work of Solomon: the foundations of splendid palaces, houses, stables, barracks, and public halls. When it was finished, it would be another city, approached by a wide road that was already completed, and girdled by a crenelated wall. Thirty thousand laborers had worked on it, as well as seventy thousand burden-bearers and eighty thousand stonecutters. From Tyre had come cedar and cypress enough for beams and roofs and paneling, for which Solomon paid an annuity of twenty thousand measures of wheat and twenty vats of oil. From Tyre, also, King Hiram had sent his servant, Huram-abi, a skilled metalworker, who, with a team of Phoenician craftsmen, had cast all the bronze required for the Temple.

As the procession approached the foot of Mount Moriah, this man was brought down from the buildings and approached the king. He made obeisance, and Solomon raised him up, embraced him, and kissed him on the cheek. About Huram-abi's neck the king hung a triple chain of gold, and into his hand he gave a tablet which confirmed him as a royal officer, with a house, land and provisions from the king's household.

They moved on, between solid ranks of people and a forest of waving palm fronds. They ascended the sloping road, passing through the wide space that would eventually be a gateway, passing the unfinished Hall of the Forest of Lebanon—so called because its columns would be forty-five immense cedar trunks, smooth and polished, soaring to the roof of oiled cedar—and opposite it the lofty stone Hall of Judgment, as yet roofless but showing its noble dimensions. And thus, at last, they came into the forecourt of the Temple, and up to the doors of the House of God.

At the portals stood two columns, made by Huram-abi, of cast bronze six times the height of a man from their bases to their great capitals, decorated with lilies and with pomegranates. That upon the right was called Jachin, that on the left was named Boaz, and both had been dedicated with the blood of sacrificial victims to uphold the porch. Between them the rays of the morning sun streamed into the Temple so that, as in a mist of gold, appeared the huge bronze laver standing upon twelve carved oxen, the lampstands, the altar for burnt offerings dwarfing any that had ever been made before, the gold-inlaid floor, the carvings of flowers and gourds and palm trees and cherubs that seemed to move and waver in the mysterious dimness. Marvel upon marvel there was, until the eye could not absorb them all.

Slowly, but with a joyous step, Solomon went up between the pillars and stood there for an instant. He was conscious of an edge of sorrow in his happiness, thinking to himself, If only David, my father, could be here to see. But then, he thought, each man who takes on himself the burden of leadership must give up that which is dearest to him; it is the sacrifice demanded of the king. As Moses was denied the sight of Canaan, so my father was denied the sight of his dream—the greatness of Israel confirmed by the House of the Lord. When we were but nomads, Yahweh dwelt within tents; now may our place among nations be secure as he is established within his House.

On that thought, he went on, and behind him pressed the chiefs and princes. So large was the Temple that there was room for all of them. Their women: wives, mothers, and daughters, went in by another door to the screened section reserved for them, for it was profanation for a woman to enter any other part of the Temple. And the multitude of Jerusalem crammed the forecourt, stood upon the walls and even upon the steps of the altars in the courtyard, climbed into the scaffolding and the empty windows of the buildings without, or filled the road, watching with a joy to match their king's as the priests carried the Ark in to its resting place.

At the far end of the Temple, folding doors of olivewood were thrown open revealing the Holy of Holies. Within the sanctuary two golden cherubs stood, ten cubits high, their vast wings touching either wall and overshadowing a space in the center. Their stern, bearded faces were lifted in warning toward the doors. The Ark was set down between them. Yet, although it was but an old, small chest of wood, it was not diminished by its surroundings; on the contrary, the cherubs, the carvings, the gold and bronze and stone all seemed to dwindle before it so that it stood alone and majestic among the tiny, transitory things made by men.

And it seemed to those who watched that the motes of the sunbeams thickened and brightened, that the mist of gold formed into a cloud. The priests backed hastily from the sanctuary, all but Zadok, who stood firm since it was his right to stand within the Holy of Holies and live. The princes, the chieftains, the great men of the land fell upon their faces. But Solomon remained standing behind Zadok, his body thrilling like a harp string struck by a master harper, suffused with the glory of the Lord. Thicker grew the cloud until the Ark could barely be seen, and now it was no longer bright but terrible and wonderful beyond measure: a Presence without shape, Formlessness containing all forms, a Nothingness that held the brilliant seed of life.

In ecstasy, Solomon cried aloud the words of the ancient oracle, and the building was so made that his voice issued from the doors and those without could plainly hear him:

> The Lord established the sun
>     in the heavens,
> But he that dwells in thick
>     darkness has spoken:
> 'Build me a house, a house
>     of habitation,
> That I may dwell therein forever.'
> Behold, it is written in the
>     Book of Jashar.

*It is accomplished!* said his heart.

He motioned with his hand, and Zadok, trembling, white-faced, harrowed and rapturous, laid hold of the doors and closed them.

Solomon turned away, facing his people, looking upon their bent backs and bowed heads. Never before had he felt himself so much the Shield of Israel, standing between them and God: he was theirs, their bond, their mediator and their bridge stretching to the power of the Lord.

Yahweh, God of my fathers, he prayed silently. I have made myself king over myself. I have taken nothing, but have dedicated myself to you for the sake of your people. When the time comes for me to make my sacrifice, to give to you what is most precious, whatsoever it may be, lend me the strength to render it willingly and with a brave heart.

Aloud, he said, "Hear, O Israel! The Lord your God, the Lord is One."

At these words, there was a rustle as all lifted their heads, and a murmur of awe that went through the Temple like the passing of wings: "Blessed be he, and blessed be his name, now and forever."

They stood up. The dedication continued: the prayers, the songs, the sacrifices. But one more thing happened which made the day even more memorable for Solomon: a gift, given him as if playfully and happily from the kind hand of God, as a father gives a honey-cake to a good child.

Word of the portent had spread quickly: how the House of the Lord had been filled with the glory of the Lord, so that the priests could not even minister but had fallen down on their faces before the cloud of glory. The whole city buzzed with the news, and "Truly, a worthy successor to our lord David!" said a thousand voices; "Truly, a king beloved of the Lord." When Solomon came out to the forecourt a thunder of hosannas greeted him.

The burnt offerings were made, and the cereal offerings, and the thank-offerings. Hundreds of oxen and sheep were slain and distributed to the people in their divisions, to eat in the booths on the first day of the Feast. Solomon and all his guests returned to the palace, where long tables had been set out under green branches in the courtyard, in the gardens, and even in the open street. Before he sat down to eat, a man was brought to him by two of the guards, a man who panted for breath and whose sweat spattered the floor.

"He came running, lord, gasping out that he had a message," said one of the guardsmen. "We hesitated to let him disturb you at the feast—"

"You have done well," said Solomon. "What is the message?"

The man opened his hand. Within it lay a heavy gold ring set with a jasper seal on which was a star.

"Sittar!" Solomon cried. "It is the ring I gave him."

"I know not, lord," said the messenger. "But he who gave it to me said that it would bring me to you without delay. He is two days' journey from Jerusalem, and he bade me say to you, 'Prepare the room you spoke of. The queen of Sheba, and your friend, her brother, will hold you to your promise.'"

On the third day of the festival, before sunset, the caravan of the Shebans arrived at Jerusalem. Because the city was so full, Solomon commanded them to make their camp on the hill above Hinnom, and a house belonging to Benaiah, which stood near the palace, was made ready for the use of the queen and her suite. As for Sittar, Solomon determined that he should lodge in the palace in the room which had formerly been his.

Sittar came to him that very evening, before dinner. The two friends embraced, and then held each other by the elbows, each inspecting the other.

"By my hand," said Solomon, "you have grown. You are as heavy as a wrestler."

Sittar had indeed become stouter, his face was fuller and his mustache and beard thicker and coarser, but his eyes still sparkled with an irrepressible spirit of levity.

He patted Solomon's arms, and said, "You, too, have grown. But into a king. Is it proper that I should jest with a king?"

"Be silent! Can you not see how my counselors frown at our laughter?" Solomon looked past him. "But you are alone. Where is your sister, the queen?"

"She would not come before Solomon in haste, but said that on the morrow she would enter the city with her gifts. In any case, she is never hungry . . . unlike her brother. I swear, I have not eaten one honest, full meal since I departed from Marib."

"What a man will not do for friendship," said Solomon. "Come, then, the feast is ready."

They sat down, all together, and ate. Sittar and Solomon shared the same bowl, and pressed the best slices of meat upon each other with much laughter and many jests. When they were done, the king took his friend's arm and led him up the stairs to the rooftop. They sat down side by side on the parapet, and Solomon said, drawing a deep breath, "It is good to see you again. I cannot tell you how good."

"Yes . . . is it not strange? The years have dropped away; it is as if we parted only yesterday. Yet I know it is not so, for word of my cousin's doings has come to us. The great new harbor at Ezion-geber, the copper mines, the new cities: the fame and wealth of Israel are the talk of the world." He looked affectionately at Solomon, and added, "I will tell you the truth. It was in my mind to wonder how the king would greet me."

"You doubted me?"

"A throne can change a man. But I saw at once that I was mistaken. What I found to love in my cousin are those very qualities which have made him great. The gods have blessed you with wisdom, Solomon."

"Not the gods, Sittar, but Yahweh alone."

"Whichever you will," Sittar said, cheerfully. "It is all one to me. Now, I pray you, tell me all that is new with you, and make the story as long as you like."

After a couple of hours of talk, they were both hoarse. They hardly realized this, however, until the glow of a lamp shone at the stairhead, and a moment after, Zabud appeared holding a light. Behind him came Abishag, with a wineskin slung over her shoulder, and bearing two goblets and a dish of honey-cakes.

"Forgive your servant, my lord," she said. "Wine makes friends more light-hearted. I will leave it here and go."

"No, no," Sittar cried, jumping to his feet. "Do not go. I am weary of looking into the ugly face of a man."

Abishag smiled at him. She set down the dish and poured wine for them. "I cannot remain," she said. "My lord knows it would be unfitting for a maiden to share the talk of men."

Solomon took her hand and pressed it. "My sister is wise," he said. "These Shebans are with maidens as wolves among the lambs."

"Your sister?" said Sittar. "I did not know—"

"She is not my father's daughter, but she is very near my heart," Solomon said, tenderly. "Without her, I should find it hard to rule." He glanced at his friend's face, the buttery light of the lamp picking out the curve of his cheek and the threads of his beard. Between these two people, dearest to him of any, he felt an utter contentment; Yahweh had no more to give him.

Abishag drew her hand away. "If my lord will permit me to go—"

"Go with my thanks, Abishag, for the wine. Zabud, take the lamp and light her down."

"As my lord commands."

The armor-bearer went before her and her body was silhouetted for an instant against the light, which pierced her robes. Sittar sighed.

"So this is the beloved of whom you told me—the fair Shunammite?" he said.

Solomon's cheeks grew hot. "No, no. She is not my beloved. I love her as a sister, nothing more. Believe me, my cousin, she is wiser than most men, she sees deep. She has been my right hand during these four years."

"I see." Sittar twisted up his mustache with a chuckle. "She is nothing more to you than a sage old man. By Ilmuqa, by the very face of Ilmuqa, my cousin, I am tempted to become an Israelite. In my own country we have no such fair and delicious advisers."

"I am in earnest, Sittar," Solomon said, with a tinge of vexation.

The prince clapped him lightly on the shoulder. "And how does my cousin know," he said, "that I also am not in earnest?"

They could not see each other save as pale blurs in the starlight, and yet both laughed suddenly at the same instant.

"You were ever one to mock," Solomon said. "But—let us talk of this another time."

He drank deeply of the cool, sweet, faintly resinous wine, and in a little while he, at least, had forgotten Abishag.

Solomon was prepared for Balkis to be lovely, to be gracious, charming and intelligent: all those things Sittar had told him of. But he was not prepared for her to be a queen. All the lands which fringed the borders of Israel were ruled by men, and he had never seen a woman who was herself the receptacle of a goddess, who stood between her people and their Deity as he with his.

He received her in his throne room, seated upon his throne of ivory. This throne stood upon a dais with six steps, and its arms were golden lions, and pairs of golden lions stood on each step with their mouths open as if roaring the glory of the king. On either side of him were ranked his counselors, bearded and grave, Benaiah and his captains, and the princes his brothers. Joel the son of Abner stood at the foot of the dais with a drawn sword, and about the walls were guardsmen, in whose golden shields the whole room was reflected, blurred as if seen through a morning mist.

Trumpets sounded Balkis' arrival, and the double doors of the throne room were opened. The king's steward, Ahushai the son of Asaph, struck the floor with his staff and said, "Behold the queen of Sheba, Mesha, and Sephar, the daughter of Merisamis."

There entered first a double file of Sheban soldiers in brazen helmets and straight tunics, girdled with belts of brass, that fell to their knees. Behind them came lines of veiled women dressed in rich robes, surrounding a litter borne by six brawny men. The bearers set the litter down before the throne and stood aside. Sittar came forward and knelt, and Balkis placed her hand on his shoulder; thus aided, she stepped from the litter. She stood perfectly still, her hands to her sides, and on her face a look of such utter detachment that she seemed no more than an image made of ivory, enamel, and precious stones. Her eyes were painted so that they appeared larger; her dark hair was covered with a veil of golden gauze sewn with pearls. From neck to ankles she was covered with a close-fitting robe of blue linen heavily worked with silver thread in leaves and flowers, and over it a mantle of blue samite encrusted with golden suns. On her head was a tall golden crown made like a sun-disk, horned, and set with gems. Beneath this heavy crown she neither swayed nor trembled, holding her head erect as if unconscious of any weight, and this added to her majesty and to the quality of unreality that clothed her.

Solomon, sitting as rigidly, with his hands resting on his thighs, caught his breath. He was not conscious of her beauty but of her strangeness: she was unnatural, like a work of art. Through his mind flashed the phrase: "You shall not pay homage to a graven image . . ."

He glanced sideways, quickly, at Sittar, who still knelt with his face upturned and a small smile on his lips. The strangeness was dispelled, a little, and he thought, She is after all no more than a woman in royal garb, his sister, as my sister Tamar was to me.

Then, to do her honor, he rose and slowly descended the six steps to stand before her. "The queen of Sheba is welcome in Israel," he said.

In a low, musical voice, she replied, "The son of David is gracious."

He became aware that the painted eyes were full of curiosity; that behind the composed mask of red-dyed lips and powdered cheeks, she was examining him with the caution of an adversary who looks out of ambush. He was at once amused by this, and looked more closely at her. He could see now that she was younger than he had thought, and that her features were delicate and perfect, although the steady stare of her eyes repelled him a little. As he watched, he could see that her chin shook with a tiny tremor, and he realized then the effort that it cost her to hold her head so still.

He said, "Will the queen sit?"

He did not wait for her answer, but motioned with his hand. A servant brought two folding chairs of olivewood, and opened them, placing cushions on each.

With an almost inaudible sigh, Balkis sat. Solomon then seated himself facing her. She said, "Let King Solomon accept the few small gifts I have brought him out of Sheba."

She lifted her hand, and porters, who had been waiting outside the doors of the throne room, now entered. They set before the dais bales of spices and herbs so that at once the whole room was filled with a sweet, savory odor; carvings of ivory, and sandalwood also, as well as goldwork, weapons with jeweled hilts, and bundles of fine cloth they placed beside the king.

Solomon nodded, smiling. "Rich are the gifts and blessed be the giver. They are accepted," he said. "My own gifts are poor indeed beside them."

At his gesture, Ahushai led out servants of the king, who placed beside the queen dishes of gold to the weight of a hundred talents, with cunningly wrought jewelry on every dish, and besides, parcels of sea-cloth from Philistia, deep purple dye from Tyre, and goblets of precious glass artfully colored.

After this ceremonial exchange, he said, "A house has been made ready for the queen. And we will dine together at sunset. But before she retires to rest and prepare herself let her make known to me what further may be done to add to her welcome."

Balkis replied, "The King has opened his hand to me so that nothing remains for me to desire, save this: let me go up to your chief temple, the fame of which I heard when I was yet two days' journey from Jerusalem, so that I may make a sacrifice there before your gods in token of the friendship between our two countries."

Solomon heard behind him a gasp from many throats. He regarded the queen impassively. He fancied that he detected a note of challenge in her voice; now that he thought of it, certainly Sittar must have told her of the God of Israel. Was it possible she asked this favor merely to place him in a quandary? For certainly it was no easy problem she set him: however he answered, he might give offense either to her or to his own people.

He said, at last, "What the queen asks is impossible. For Yahweh, our God, is a jealous god and he has forbidden women to minister to his altars or to appear before him. It is from caution that I deny the queen's request, for Yahweh might send down fire from heaven upon her, and while the queen's own goddess would doubtless protect her, surely the wrath of Yahweh would be upon me and my people."

In answering thus, he made her responsible for the safety of his own land, so that she had no recourse but to agree.

"However," he went on, "let the queen Balkis go up on the slopes of Olivet, to En-rogel to the Stone of the Serpent. There I will send her whatever beasts are necessary and there she may sacrifice to her own gods."

He heard a rustle of movement, and murmurings among his counselors. He turned his head to eye them, and said, "Let not the honored elders mutter behind their hands. If any would speak, speak now that I may hear him."

Chimham the son of Barzillai, clearing his throat and fumbling with his curly lamb's-wool beard, said, "May the king live forever. Your servant only fears that this may be an insult in the eyes of Israel and Judah as they keep the Feast of Booths, to see the smoke of a foreign sacrifice go up in the sight of the House of the Lord. Further . . . hm, hm . . . a sacrifice to a woman's god . . ."

Solomon looked from him to the others. Some were scowling, some shook their heads, and even Benaiah had an unhappy expression on his broad face.

Then the king said, "The son of Barzillai is wise and experienced. Does he speak for himself alone, or for all?"

"For all, lord," said one, Azariah the son of Zadok, and the rest nodded their heads.

"Very well. Now let the son of Barzillai tell me: if the House of the Lord were destroyed, would the God of Israel also be destroyed?"

Chimham looked shocked. "My lord—" he began.

"Then," Solomon continued, "the House of God is not God. And although our God dwells among us in the Temple, yet tell me, does he see only Jerusalem or does he see all Israel?"

"He sees all Israel, blessed be his name."

"And does he see also into the land of Moab, and even into the land of Egypt?"

Chimham said, in puzzlement, "He who made the earth sees to the uttermost corners of the earth, my lord."

"That is so. Yet, although he sees the altars of Ashtarte in Tyre, and the altars of Ra and Osiris in Egypt, he does not smite the Phoenicians nor the Egyptians. Why is this, son of Barzillai?"

"I—truly I do not know, my lord," Chimham stammered.

"Why, wherein is it written that we are to forbid to other peoples their own worship or their own gods? Only to us, his people, is it commanded, 'You shall have no other gods beside me.' It is we, alone, who are chosen of the Lord. Or is this not so, son of Barzillai?"

"It is so, my lord," said Chimham submissively.

"And does the son of Barzillai—do the rest of you—imagine that to the Lord Yahweh the distance from his Temple to Tyre or to Egypt is greater than the distance to En-rogel? All the earth is but a pebble in the hand of the Lord."

He bit in the corner of his mouth to keep from smiling, for it was clear that they could not answer him. "Therefore," he said, "let all be done as I have commanded, unless—" He turned back to Balkis, and now he allowed the smile to creep out. "Unless the queen have a further objection?"

He saw her mouth twitch. She rose, and said, "Happy are these your servants who stand before you continually and hear your wisdom, son of David. I am satisfied with your decision. I will go up to this place you have named and offer a sacrifice there to Shams—and invoke her blessing on your head."

At this, there came a positive groan of terror from some of the old men. But Solomon ignored them. He stood, and said, "If it will please the queen, let it be so."

He watched her seat herself within the litter, swinging herself in with practiced ease despite the heavy crown and tight-fitting robes. Her women assisted her, setting her mantle straight and placing cushions at her back. The bearers slung the straps about their shoulders, set the loops over the ends of the poles and heaved up the litter. At that moment, she looked sidelong at him with a slow smile.

"Until dinner, son of David," she said, and it was as if she granted him a brief truce.

But at dinner, she was another woman. She had washed the pale, ceremonial paint from her cheeks so that her skin glowed with its own honey color. Her hair was braided in tresses, and about it, over her veil, she wore a wreath of little flowers made most cunningly of copper and silver. Her dress was cut full in the sleeves and skirt, with three flounces all embroidered in colored thread; the women of Solomon's household who were at the table gazed at it from the corners of their eyes. There was nothing of the cold and distant queen about her any longer; she was gay and winning, full of jests and ready to laugh, bending now toward Solomon, now toward Sittar, who sat upon her other side, and eating with relish of the many delicacies with which the table was covered.

Solomon was utterly charmed, so that he could not look at her enough. He took opportunity to say, as they were washing their hands after the roast meats had been cleared away, "It is my hope that the queen will make her visit a long one."

"Oh," she replied, "the king must first say what beauties there are in his land for him to show me."

"Little to match that which has come to me out of Sheba," he answered. "Nevertheless, this is a fair land which our God has given us. There are here both high and low places, snowy peaks and fertile valleys. I will show the queen the wonder of the Sea of Salt and the chalk plains above it, whiter than the moon. And there is winding Jordan, which flows down from the Lake of the Harp between green meadows, woodlands, and desolate cliffs. There are dark forests of oaks, wide grasslands flowing like a sea, vineyards where a single bunch of grapes is a load for two men . . ."

She smiled, and said, "Rich indeed is this land in the love of its king. Well, you may show me what you will."

She watched him covertly as he took up an orange and began to peel it. He rested his elbows on the table, his head bent and a little inclined to one side, intent upon his task; his long musician's fingers, strong and nervous, stripped off the rind, which threw golden lights upon his brown skin. A worthy antagonist, she thought to herself. Sittar was right, he is a man and a king. This is not such a one as Hadad to be led on a halter . . . better for me if he were put down and another, easier to deal with, in his place.

She glanced at Andonijah, who sat halfway down the board. He was eating grapes, two and three at a mouthful, and spitting the seeds on the cloth before him. Beside him, Nebat the son of Ahijah lounged, yawning languidly and toying with a cup. The two together put her in mind of some great shaggy hunting dog companioned with a lazy leopard; but who, she wondered, was their master—the king, some other, or were they masterless? Looking about, her attention was caught by Joab, who was seated opposite Adonijah, eating very frugally, no more than a mouthful of bread and cheese. The heavy-lidded Bedouin eyes were upon the prince and there was a half-smile, almost of contempt, on Joab's face. As she watched him, his eyes flickered toward her, cold and dangerous, appraising, even scornful. She had been introduced to him earlier; she knew the name, not only from Hadad's tales, but from Sittar's account of the conflict between the king and his brother. This was one to watch, one who, if she was not wary, might upset all plans for the sake of his own ends.

The servants brought honey-cakes and sesame-cakes, and poured a rich, dark, sweet wine. Benaiah was telling the tale of how he had gone down into the pit to slay the lion, speaking in his slow, modest way; the story was well known to most of those present, but he had been urged to tell it again for the sake of the Egyptian and Syrian envoys. At the other end of the table, Abishag chatted with Solomon's two wives, the Egyptian princess, Tuosri, daughter of Psusennes, and Mahalath the Sidonitess, the niece of Hiram of Tyre. Bathsheba sat there also, watching her son and the queen of Sheba with a confusion of emotions: pride that he was sought after by so great a monarch, and resentment that he should pay so close a court to a foreign woman. As if, she thought, we had not enough foreigners already in the house. And she turned, and over her shoulder spoke sharply to one of the servants, who moved too slowly with the wine jar.

Solomon had fallen into a reverie, resting his chin upon the fork of thumb and forefinger, looking at Balkis and her brother as they conversed together beside him. In both faces the same liveliness showed, the same spark of amusement at life itself, her fine and tawny profile against his darker, rounder face, like amber upon sandalwood. Absently, the king hummed to himself, a snatch of melody that wound into his mind; he touched his finger to the table and heard in his imagination the answering sound of a chord. It was long since he had composed a song, and suddenly, with the profile of Balkis before him, words fitted together to follow the gentle weaving of the melody:

> Rise, my love; my beautiful one
> > come away.
> Let me see your form, let me hear
> > your voice,
> For your voice is sweet and your
> > form is comely.

Balkis turned to him abruptly. "What said the son of David?"

He started. He had unconsciously spoken the last few words aloud. "Nothing," he said. "A sudden, passing thought." And then he smiled, sitting straighter and reaching for the dish of fruit. "I will tell it you one day, perhaps," he said.

The eighth day of the Feast of Booths had passed. The people returned to farms and flocks, the slopes about Jerusalem were empty save for grazing sheep, and the city returned to its normal ways.

Each morning, an hour before noon, if there were any suits of law or special pleas to be heard, Solomon sat in judgment, and on the morning after the festival ended, he went as usual to the throne room, for the Hall of Judgment which he was building upon Moriah was not yet finished. Queen Balkis had asked to be present, out of curiosity, she said, to see how such matters were dealt with among the Israelites, and when the king took his place upon his throne, she made herself comfortable in a large carved and cushioned chair nearby. At the foot of the throne sat a scribe before his little table; on the floor beside Balkis sat one of her own servants with papyrus, reed pens and ink, to make notes for her.

The first case was dull and long, involving grazing rights and the use of land, and taking in two whole villages, one of Ephraim and one of Gilead, which faced each other across the Jordan. But the second case made Balkis sit up attentively; she tapped her scribe on the shoulder and bade him write down everything that was said.

This suit concerned two women: one the widow of a Benjamite, the other a Moabitess of loose morals who dwelt in the same house. These two came and stood before the throne, and behind them was an official of the city who, with an expression like that of a man who feels yesterday's wine fighting in his stomach, was holding an extremely small and dirty baby wrapped in a sheepskin. The women were slatternly and poorly dressed, although the Moabitess had a kind of savage handsomeness.

"What is the plea?" said Solomon.

The official cleared his throat. Before he could utter a word, the woman of Benjamin said swiftly, "O king, live forever. This woman has a room in my house, neither of us having husbands and being therefore alone together, except upon certain occasions . . . and I gave birth to a child while she was in the house. Then on the third day after I was delivered, this woman also gave birth to a child. But the child of this woman died in the night because she lay upon it."

"Liar! Whore!" shrieked the Moabitess. "It is false!"

"Be silent," said Ahushai the steward, who stood on the lowest step of the dais, holding his staff of office.

"Let the daughter of Benjamin continue," said Solomon. "Then we shall hear the other one."

"She lay upon it and killed it," the Benjamite repeated, firmly. "Then she arose in the middle of the night and took my child from my side and laid her dead child on my bosom. Thus when I arose toward morning to nurse my child, behold it was dead, but when I came to examine it closely it was not the child I had borne." She looked bitterly at the other woman, and with tears starting to her eyes, said, "My lord sees that I have nothing but my child. I pray you, return it to me."

The Moabitess burst in fiercely, "She lies, she lies! My lord king, may my tongue wither if I be not telling the truth. As the king is wiser than all other men, so he can look into the hearts of liars. She lay upon her own baby in the night and killed it, and when in the morning she found it dead she pretended that my child was hers." And she, too, began to weep.

"The living child is mine!" cried the woman of Benjamin. She turn on the other with her hands half raised as if to claw. The Moabitess snarled like a cat, and spat at her.

Ahushai thrust his staff between them. "Silence!" he said angrily. "You forget that you stand before the king, your lord."

Solomon twisted the point of his beard thoughtfully between thumb and forefinger. Balkis was leaning forward to watch him with a mocking smile, and even the guardsmen, who stood at ease leaning on their shields in the corners, were grimacing and winking to each other as secretly as they could.

The official, in a pitiful tone, said, "My lord, I pray you decide between these two, as your servant has been holding this child for an hour . . ."

Solomon could not help a twitch of mirth. Then he said, "The matter is easily settled. There are no witnesses; it is the word of one against another. Each of you says that the living child is hers. And each is a woman modest and honest, unwilling to bring false testimony before your king."

Both women bowed their heads.

Solomon turned to the nearest of the guardsmen. "Come hither," he said. "Draw your sword. Take the child and cut it in two."

The soldier drew his long, straight sword; then, as the significance of the king's words penetrated his mind, he stopped and stared open-mouthed at his master.

Solomon's face had become hard, his eyes bleak as crystal. "Why do you tarry?" he snapped. "Do you imagine I am given to jesting?" He looked at the two women icily. "Since the child belongs to both, let each have half."

The guardsman swallowed. He was a seasoned fighter, and in war would kill a child without a second thought, but this seemed to him cold-blooded and too deliberate for his liking. The king's features were set like stone, however, so he took a deep breath, went up to the official, and said, "Put the child down so that I may strike."

The throne room was as silent as death. Even Balkis was, for the moment, stricken white-faced, for it was clear that what the king said, he would perform.

The soldier, with one more glance at the king, raised his sword. And suddenly, the woman of Benjamin cried out, "Oh, my lord— stop him! I lied! Let the king punish me as he will. The child is hers. Give it to her—only do not slay it."

The king looked at the Moabitess. "What says the other?"

She twisted her fingers together. "Your maidservant has heard the king's word. Let his will be done. It shall be neither mine nor hers. Divide it."

Solomon clapped his hands. The hardness had fallen from his face; he laughed like a boy. "You have settled it between you," he said. "Give the child to the Benjamite, for her mother's heart has spoken for her son. As for the woman of Moab, put her forth from the city. And be thankful," he added, with an edge to his voice, "that the king is merciful and does not have you flogged as you deserve."

The woman of Benjamin snatched up her child from the floor and with tears streaming down her face bowed to the king. The official, holding his damp garments away from his body, conducted both women from the throne room.

Balkis was looking at Solomon with a curious expression, and she said, "The report which I heard in my own land of your affairs and your wisdom was true, but I would not believe it until I came and saw with my own eyes. The half was not told me; the son of David surpasses all that I heard."

Throughout the room there were broad grins; the tale would spread through the soldiers' barracks and through the city like fire in dry grass.

"I am grateful for the queen's good opinion," said Solomon, flushing with pleasure. "If there are no more suits to be heard, let us refresh ourselves."

But just then a door at the rear of the room opened, and a servant said, "The lady Bathsheba enters."

Solomon rose as his mother came in, thinking that she must have been listening to the case and was coming either to praise or to scold him. His face was already set in lines of resignation to either one, as she approached and bowed.

He went down from the throne and bent his head before her. Ahushai brought her a chair and she sat at the king's right hand.

She said, "Well is it that my son has not yet risen from giving judgment, for I am here as a supplicant."

He lifted his eyebrows. "Is it possible—?"

"A small request I am about to make of you," she went on. "Do not refuse me."

"Ask, my mother, for I will not refuse you."

"I have come to plead the suit of your brother, Adonijah," she said. She glanced involuntarily at the door through which she had entered, and following her eyes Solomon saw that Adonijah had come in quietly and was standing in the doorway with his arms folded. He was dressed in dark clothing, like one who wishes to avoid attention.

Solomon's puzzlement changed to wariness. "What is your wish?" he asked, but he was not at all prepared for what followed.

"The son of Haggith came to me, asking that I serve as his matchmaker since his own mother is now dead. He prays you to give him the maiden Abishag the Shunammite as his wife. As my son knows, Adonijah bears him only good will, and it is because I am convinced of this, and of his love for the maiden, that I—that I have consented to . . ."

She had begun confidently, but before the look on her son's face she fell abruptly silent. He stared down at her, and her features blurred and swayed before him. The veins in his neck were distended and he felt as if he were choking. He fumbled with the collar of his tunic, although it was by no means tight. Then his breath returned to him; he became calmer and could think.

This was the gall his father had tasted, of whispers behind his back, of secret plottings, of trust betrayed and turned against him. In one swift rush all was clear to him: his mother would never have sided with Adonijah except for her own gain. Between them, they had hatched up this plan to deprive him of his friend. And to what other end than to weaken him?

Was it possible Adonijah really loved the girl, and desired her? It might be so, but it was certain Abishag had no inkling of it; neither did she feel for Adonijah anything but loathing. This had come from thin air, this proposal, and as such it was obvious it came from malice, to divide him from the girl.

And his own mother—it was this which hurt most, to hear her plead Adonijah's cause, out of the jealousy he now understood must move her.

He said, between his teeth, "You are kind, my mother. Why do you not ask for him the kingdom also?"

Bathsheba recoiled as if he had slapped her. She said, in a shaking voice, "Why this anger? Is the maiden so much to you? Then why do you not take her to wife yourself? Was it not enough for me to have her in the house, to have her take my husband from me at the end so that he could no longer see me but set me aside? Now she must take my son as well. What manner of viper is she? And you—who are you to disregard the word of the Lord your God: 'Honor your father and mother'? Honor! There is no honor for me any longer—I who am but a maidservant in my own house."

"Enough," Solomon said hoarsely. His hands were cold as ice, and he scarce recognized his own voice. "Am I king over Israel, or a child still, to be chidden for misdeeds? Enough, I say."

He swung round to Adonijah, who was scowling blackly. "Tell me, son of Haggith, do you love the Shunammite so dearly? Or is it Joab, once again, who has driven you to this poisoned act?"

He saw immediately that he had guessed aright. With that, his passion rose up in him. He held it in check, however, and said, with an effort, "There was once love between us, Adonijah. Did we not slay a lion together? Why, then, have you turned against me?"

"It is not I who have turned against you," Adonijah retorted harshly. "You plucked the crown from my head. If Joab incited me to proclaim myself, it was only what was in my own mind. Did not our father say to me, 'Watch over your brother'? But you have set me aside, and now you will deny me the woman as well. What is to be my portion, I, the eldest—am I to have nothing but ashes?"

He was inflexible; he understood nothing any longer save that he had been wronged. "You are blind," Solomon said. "Ask me no more for what is not mine to give. Ask, rather, of Yahweh to send you contentment."

He turned his back, still reining in his fury lest he do something rash. His mother stood before him, her face white as linen, seeing ruin and the hatred she had fanned in her son, knowing herself shut irrevocably from his life.

"Well, lady," he said bitterly, "you have fallen into pretty company. Do you not see you have been used? Let them take the Shunammite from me to satisfy your jealousy—and what will be next? Would you have me bare my throat to Adonijah's dagger?"

He swung away, mounting the steps of the dais slowly, almost painfully. At the throne, he clenched his hand on one of the lion arms, so that his seal ring bit into his finger. He sat down heavily and glared at the two below. "Leave me," he said. And then, unable longer to control himself, he roared, "Go! Clear the room. Let none stay on pain of death!"

He was not conscious of their departure. He was alone, as only a king can be, encircled by envy and rancor, which assailed him as wolves to pull him down. In this loneliness, the very air was envenomed. Then, all at once, a soft voice near at hand said, "Heavy is the crown, O my brother Solomon."

It was Balkis; he had forgotten her, nor could his command affect her. And with the thought, and with her words that linked them on the island of power, he felt no longer so alone.

He held out his hand to her. She had come up on the dais, and she clasped his hand with her own, that was cool and firm. "And you, my sister?" he said.

"I have tasted the same cup. The Threefold One, she it is who gives me strength. Otherwise, I am alone, as you are."

He nodded.

"And does my brother Solomon so much love the maiden they spoke of?"

"Surely Balkis must know that there can be a love between a man and a woman which is neither of wedlock nor desire. The maiden is dear to me as a sister. But this is not the root of the matter. She is also my friend and my adviser. Shall I give her to Adonijah for his lust, and cut off my right hand? They were fools; they should have guessed I would see to the core of their artifice."

She drew still nearer so that she was almost touching him, and a light and delicious fragrance came to his nostrils, sweet as roses, heady as wine. "As they stand below your throng they see only each other," she said. "But you, who sit high above them, can see them all. This it is to be a sovereign."

He rose up, still holding her hand, and looked down into her round, violet eyes for a long space without speaking. With a little laugh, she drew her hand away suddenly, breaking the spell. She went down a step or two, and said, "Come, you forget the duty you owe your guest. It is long past midday."

"I owe more than I can say to my guest," he replied. "Let us discourse of this again."

"Whenever you will."

With that, happiness returned to his face and he led her to the doors.

The house which Solomon had given to the queen stood behind a high, blank wall, in the midst of a small but rich garden. A great cistern of stone watered it, flowers and sweet-smelling shrubs abounded, and the trees were full of bright-plumaged birds. To this place, very late that night, came Adonijah, conducted by a dwarfish man of the queen's retinue. This man, Haran by name, came no higher than Adonijah's breastbone, but had shoulders and arms fully as powerful as those of the prince; his arms hung below his knees and gave him the appearance of an ape out of Cush. He led Adonijah into the garden, bowed; and, apelike, disappeared silently into the darkness.

Adonijah stood in the moonlight looking curiously about him. He felt no fear, but with his left hand he held his scabbard forward and ready for safety's sake. Haran had earlier brought him a message saying only, "My mistress bids you follow me, unattended, when I come for you near the middle watch of the night," and showing a ring which bore the horned sun of Sheba. Adonijah was not one to concern himself with needless speculation, but took each matter as it came. He followed Haran when he returned, and now he brushed up his beard with the back of his hand and waited for whatever might next appear.

A woman, shimmering in the moonlight, approached him. It was the queen, dressed in a pleated Egyptian gown with a broad collar and wide sleeves that left her arms bare to the elbow. Her dark hair was combed down to her shoulders and shone glossily in the pale beams. "The son of Haggith is welcome," she said, in a low voice. With a gesture, she indicated that he should sit upon the edge of the cistern, and when he had done so she sat beside him, a little distance apart.

"I sent for the son of Haggith to meet me here," she said, "because what is spoken within walls is soon heard by all the house."

He said nothing, but waited, playing idly with the hilt of his dagger, and admiring her appearance. He had three concubines, famous for their beauty, and yet the queen outshone them all. At the same time, she made him uneasy, as Joab did, for he felt that there were in all her words hidden meanings.

"A stranger in a strange land is sometimes puzzled," she said, "by the surfaces of things, as one who had never seen a bronze mirror might wonder in what depths of it lay the face she saw. By some such wonder was I taken this morning in the hall of judgment. Perhaps the prince, Adonijah, can explain it to me?"

"Explain? What is there to explain?" he said, somewhat bewildered.

"Why, who does not know that of two young lions it is the stronger who rules, taking the lionesses for his own and hunting where he pleases? So it is among men in the lands where there are kings, although not in Sheba where a woman rules. And in Israel I see it is not so. Here, I have seen the strong cowed by the weak, the elder chided by the younger, the powerful man subdued by the crafty. Odd, indeed, are the ways of your country!"

"He is the king," Adonijah said, sullenly.

"Yes . . . he is the king. But does no blood of David flow in your veins?" She raised a hand to check his answer. "But there—I misjudge your customs, again. Perhaps here it is the youngest who must by law take the throne?"

"He won it by guile. But I do not see—"

"I thought as much," Balkis interrupted. "By guile, the resort of the weakling. The common folk will think it wisdom, but we who rule know it for mere jackal cunning. Why, think! I have seen the kings of other lands—Psusennes, who holds the scepter of the Nile, Khanum who rules Ophir, Pinhas of Ethiopia—these are strong men, men of might like yourself. When Solomon denied you the woman you wanted, he whined and scolded. Pharaoh would have slain you out of hand. And you yourself? If you sat upon the throne, would you have done no more than he did?"

Adonijah tightened his hand upon his dagger. Goaded by her words, stung, yet baffled by her intention, he snarled, "Well do you know I would have cut him down. Listen to me, daughter of Merisamis. I am none of your subtle-tongued intriguers but a plain man. The throne should have been mine—it was mine by right! You see me here helpless, bound hand and foot, and you mock at me. Why? How is this your concern? Did you summon me to make sport of me? As God lives, if you were a man—"

She bent forward, touching his arm lightly. "No, no. Believe me, I meant no mockery. I think only of the welfare of my own land. And it would be very much to my advantage to have a strong man, not a weakling, on the throne of Israel."

He stared at her, wrinkling his brow. "No more of this," he said at last. "Speak plainly, or by my hand I will listen no more."

She appraised him with a half-smile; then she said, "Very well. Sheba is rich, with slaves and gold and spices. Nevertheless, we have few warriors, for my people are clansmen who live far apart and can only with difficulty be brought out of their villages for battle. If I could carry my wealth freely to the Great Sea, and if I could have at my side an ally who does not fear war and who leads spearmen and swordsmen as bold as himself—there is no limit to the empire that might be ruled. I came here searching for such a man. Solomon is not he."

Adonijah licked his lips. "An empire?" he said.

"Greater than Asshur. To join my golden city, Marib, across the wilderness and across Edom with the city of Jerusalem. To strike hard and sudden against Tyre, and subdue it, and so win the seaports. Then Aram . . . and then against Egypt itself. But such a man must be a lion, to take my hand and go with me against the world."

He laughed harshly. "As God sees me," he said, "I was ever a fighter. It is what I was born to. But the queen speaks as if Solomon could be brushed aside like a feather. It is not so easy. It calls for time. He is much loved, and there are far too many who will follow him."

Balkis rose, and he stared up at her, his breath coming more quickly at the cool, silver smoothness of her.

"I have a plan," she said. "Let me weaken him further, confusing his mind and his senses, making him blind and unwary. It may be I can drive a wedge between him and his friends. You, meantime, may gather some strength about you and make sure of those who will uphold your cause. Then, when it comes to a conflict between you, I have a weight to cast in the scales."

"Ah? What is that?"

She touched the horned, golden disk upon her breast. "Can I trust you to be silent? I have made an alliance with Hadad the son of Hadar. He is in Edom even now, raising an army. When I send this amulet to him, he will march with his soldiers to support you. Thus will you gain the throne."

Adonijah chuckled. "The dog of Edom, eh? So he has returned to his kennel? That is a word which would make my peaceful brother quake if he but knew it."

"He must not know it. None knows it—not my own brother—none save Hadad and myself, and now, you. And it is in my mind that when the Edomite has served his turn he may be thrust aside lest he prove troublesome. He is a schemer—not a man, not the man for an alliance with me. Well, prince? You must yourself answer the question. Are you that man?"

He sprang up, towering above her. He would have seized her in his arms, but there was such an aura of queenliness about her that he was intimidated. He stood for an instant in doubt, and then he grinned and said, "I am. And let the queen remember that there can be more than hands clasped in an alliance. I am as apt in the bedchamber as upon the battlefield."

She regarded him coldly, her eyes full of moonlight. "You are indeed daring," she replied. "We will talk of that when you sit upon the throne. Go, now. Remember, be silent and secret, and prepare yourself."

She held out her hand, and after a moment he took it and kissed it. She went with him to the gate, and when he hesitated, she said, "Quickly! Who knows what eyes may be watching, even here? I promise you, I will not be deaf to sweet words when all is won. But he is a fool who spends his money before it is earned. Farewell, king's son. You will soon be a king."

She thrust him through and closed the gate. Then she leaned back against the wall, laughing silently. She looked up at the bland, calm face of the moon and slowly her mirth died within her. The thought of Solomon rose to plague her: a hundred details of his speech, his appearance, his manner, like summer midges biting. She had called him guileful and weak, but it was clear to her he was neither; he was worth a hundred such as Adonijah. Doubt stirred in her, uncertainty of what had seemed so sure and simple a course.

Then she shook out her hair in the night breeze, gathering again her divided resolution, steeling herself to that which she had planned, and thus she returned to the house.

Adonijah, when he left her, blew out a long breath. I must have wine, he thought, and a woman to ease me of the fire she has kindled in me. Fragments of her words whirled in his head—thoughts of empire, of power and wealth, and of Balkis herself lovelier than any other prize. He started for his own house, but when he had come to the end of the wall that bounded the garden a whisper made him pause.

"My lord!" The voice came from the top of the wall.

On the motion of looking up, he had drawn his dagger. A bulky, dark shape slid down to the road before him: the dwarf, Haran. He bowed low before Adonijah, touching the ground with his forehead.

"What would you?" said Adonijah.

"My lord, fear nothing. I am unarmed. Let me but ask my lord—"

"Well?"

The dwarf, on his knees, lifted his round, flat, thick-lipped face. "Is it true that the god of the Israelites is a man?"

"He is no man, but a being who is eternal."

"Ah, but my lord, you say 'he.' Then he is not one of the Accursed Ones, the Threefold Goddess of these Shebans—not a woman."

"No. Are you no Sheban?"

"I am an Ophirite, my lord. I was betrayed by a woman I trusted, captured in a raid, and sold into slavery among the Shebans. In my land, we sacrifice to Warah', the Shining Lord, whom the desert men call Sin, but in Sheba he is no more than the consort of their accursed Shams, slain as a goat every seven years and torn to pieces that his blood may make their fields fertile. Now, my lord, I pray you, tell me is it true that the law of the Israelites gives sanctuary to an escaped slave?"

Adonijah nodded. "Our law is, if a slave escapes into this land he is not to be turned over to his master but may live among us in peace, so long as he abide by the laws of Israel. And you—"

The dwarf hitched toward him on his knees. "Great lord," he said, holding his palms together, "Haran has been a slave for nine years. It is bitter bread, the bread of slavery, and more bitter when eaten in a land where a goddess rules men. I can be of service to you, lord, if you will free me and give me sanctuary in your land."

Adonijah regarded him with distaste. "How can you be of service to me?"

The dwarf's voice fell almost to a whisper. "My lord, put no trust in the Sheban queen. She is more quick and deadly than the desert viper. Her goddess hates all those lands which are ruled by kings in the name of a god. She will give you fair words—even as she did tonight—and betray you."

"You heard all that we said?"

"I heard, my lord. I am silent as the burial cave. Only, remember that Haran will serve you, he will be your eye and ear and hand within her house."

Adonijah lifted his dagger, uneasily. Was it wise to let live a witness to what had been spoken between himself and the queen? Then he paused. Who could trust a woman, after all?

He said, "Very well. We shall see. Serve me, and I will give you your freedom. But if you mean treachery, little man, be certain I will cut out your living heart and eat it before your very eyes."

The dwarf fell upon his face and kissed Adonijah's sandal. "My lord, you are kind, you will not regret it," he said. Then he leaped up, ran a few steps, and gave a spring; his long arms swung and he caught the coping of the wall. In an instant, he had vanished into the shadows of the foliage as if he had never been.

# IV THE SONG

Nathan the prophet had seen more than fourscore years pass him by. Now, at the age of eighty-seven, he lived in a tiny hut upon the shoulder of the mountain of God, at Gibeon, no longer going forth save at daybreak, when he climbed to the high place to see the sun rise and to say his morning prayers. Pilgrims coming to the holy mount visited him to ask his blessing; the Gibeonites brought him bread and curds so that he wanted for nothing. The fire was dying in him, and he was content to be an old man, dozing in the sun, feeling himself near to God, whose love sustained and nourished him, and whose voice he heard infrequently, nowadays, as if the time for warnings was past.

But a word came to him that awoke him. It was borne by travelers, whenever he asked after the king: "Our lord the king is well, but if you would see him you must seek after the Sheban queen." More and more often was it told how the king spent his time with his guest, how they rode out together, not only in chariots but on horseback, the queen riding a horse as if she were a man, which was a shameful thing to see. The business of the kingdom was neglected; the king put off all affairs, judgments, and councils, on the plea that he must show courtesy to his visitor and let her see his domain.

When he heard this, Nathan was filled with sorrow and anger. Yet he was old and weary and had no wish to travel the steep miles to Jerusalem, and each day when he sat before his door looking out over the hills he grew drowsy: the pains in his joints eased as the sun warmed him, and he said to himself, "Tomorrow."

But one morning he went up, as usual, to stand near the bronze

altar that had been built on the high place by Bezalel the son of Uri
in days gone by, and he began to say the first prayer, when suddenly the sky darkened before his eyes. Fire lanced down from
heaven and touched the altar, and thunder rumbled above Gibeon,
and the voice of God said within the thunder, "Where is my servant,
Nathan? Has he departed this life that he no longer speaks against
wickedness? Or does he fear the wrath of the king? Woe to him, if he
set his age or his king above the wrath of the Lord God."

Nathan bowed his head. The thunder died away in ominous
grumbles, the sky cleared once more. The old man took up his staff,
wrapped half a loaf of bread in a cloth, and without even finishing
his prayers set out on the dusty road to the city.

Solomon was only vaguely aware of the gossip that flew from
mouth to mouth. These days, he was like a drunkard who is blind
and deaf to all save the allure of wine, steeping himself in wine,
forgetting to eat, unable to sleep for thinking of more wine, ever
drinking and never sated. And this wine which he imbibed was a
glorious drink, for it never palled on him nor surfeited him: its
variety was infinite and its pleasure always new. Nor was he aware
of his enslavement; he did not know that he was in love, but thought
only that to be with Balkis, to speak to her, to look at her was a
delight that shortened the days into one day, into the single hour of
*now* when he was with her, and lengthened intolerably all that time
when he was not at her side.

They had made several journeys, to visit the vineyards at the
Brook of Eshcol, to look upon the Salt Sea and the ghostly chalk
cliffs below Jericho, and to inspect the immense new stables at
Megiddo. He had learned to his joy that Balkis could not only drive
a chariot like a man but could ride a horse, and he had given her a
superb Egyptian mare, slender of neck, with a small head, shiny-
black as pitch, swift and tireless. Then they began to ride out together each day from Jerusalem—except upon the Sabbath—at first
with no other attendants than his armor-bearer Zabud and a couple
of her soldiers; then, alone, in spite of the entreaties of Benaiah, of
Joel the son of Abner, and of the captain of the queen's bodyguard, a
wiry, bowlegged man named Arunazel. In the end Joel and Arunazel, who had taken to each other from the first, arranged to send six
men, three Pelethites and three Shebans, to follow the king and
queen each day, keeping a good distance from the two but never
letting them out of sight.

One day, Solomon and Balkis rode out along the Vale of Kidron,

northward toward the high mountain village of Ramah, where
Solomon had a summer house. It was a cool morning with a fresh
breeze that puffed feathers of cloud across the sky and set the plumes
of their horses' caparisons nodding and snapping. Solomon's spirits
were high, and as they rode he sang aloud a mountaineers' song:
"Turn, turn, O maiden, turn that we may gaze on you."

"The heart of my friend is merry today," said Balkis.

"Wherefore not?" he replied, laughing. "Is it not blithe to ride free
as a bird, to be winged, to smell the mountain wind and have no
cares?"

"Is it so? Has the king no cares, then?"

"Call me not 'king' this morning, I pray you," he said. "I have set
aside that heavy mantle for these few days. I will not think of cares;
there will be time enough for that when . . ." He paused. And when
she looked at him, he went on, "When my sister, Balkis, feels that she
must return to her own place. I would that day might be put off
forever."

"We need not think of that now," she said. "I, too, have put away
my cares. Tell me, rather, what that great rock is that looms above us
where the road climbs?"

He said, "It is called the Stone of Meeting, for at it this northern
road meets those which come from Gibeah and Gibeon. At its sum-
mit there is a hill track branching off; we will leave the road and
take it."

"Let us make haste, then," she said, "lest those cares we seek to
escape catch us up. *Hai!* my little Orab is restless, she is athirst and
looks for the mountain streams."

With that, she clapped her heels into the mare and urged her
forward. The flat, round cap she wore blew off, and her hair
streamed out like the wings of a raven. With a shout, Solomon galloped after her, and bending far over from the saddle scooped up
her cap and bore it with him.

They dashed up the road, the dust rising behind them in a great
cloud. The road bent round the foot of the steep, ribbed face of rock
which towered on their right hand, bleak and gray. Balkis looked
over her shoulder at Solomon, laughing, and then suddenly her mare
checked, reared up neighing, and almost fell. From behind the angle
of the rock a tall old man had stepped directly into her path, holding
out a knotty staff to bar her way. With some difficulty, Balkis kept
her seat, reined in her mount and gentled it, and then looked fiercely
at the intruder.

He was burnt almost black from the sun, hard and dry as a

mummy, his flesh shriveled to cords, his white hair hanging below his bent shoulders and tangling in his coarse beard. But his eyes glared into hers with such wildness that for a moment she was deprived of speech. In that moment, Solomon joined her.

He said, "Long is it since I have beheld Nathan the prophet. Yet it would be better for him to come to me in my palace, rather than to stop me like a highwayman by the roadside."

Nathan leaned on his staff, and retorted, "Little have I to do with palaces, O king. I come and I go where Yahweh sends me. Nor will the son of David escape the eye of the Lord either within his palace or upon the roadside. For the Lord God will come upon you unawares, like a highwayman, to call on you to stand and deliver over to him your charge, the care of Israel. How will you answer him, son of David?"

Solomon answered, quietly, "That is between my God and myself."

"Pride, pride!" cried the prophet, in a ringing voice. "Be not deceived in yourself, man of Judah. Solomon is not above the Law of God, given to our fathers upon Sinai. 'If anyone entices you, saying, "Let us go and serve alien gods," you must not yield to him nor heed him; you must not show him mercy, nor spare him—your own hand must be first against him to put him to death!' So says the Law. Woe to you, O king, if you break the covenant you and your father made with the Lord God, to follow his commandments and to walk in his ways."

Solomon listened patiently, although Nathan filled him with annoyance, and he thought, Never does he open his mouth save to croak warnings of doom. Has my mother perhaps incited him to follow me here and cry out against Balkis, also, in her jealousy?

Balkis said sternly, "Why do you permit this madman to speak thus to you? Ride him down, and let us go."

Nathan's eyes blazed at her. "Woman of Sheba," he said, "be silent. Thus has it come to pass in Israel that an alien speaks before the face of the Lord's anointed." He turned his hot gaze on Solomon. "Beware, son of David. Go not whoring after strangers and their abominations. The voice of God speaks through me, saying, 'I put before you a blessing and a curse; a blessing if you heed my commands, and a curse if you do not heed them but run after alien gods.'"

"I have heard all that Nathan has said," Solomon replied, putting his hand on the bridle of Balkis' mare, to hold her still. "Be assured I will take careful thought of it. Let him also remember that it is the queen of Sheba of whom he speaks; unwise and discourteous is he who offends a guest. Now let us pass."

Nathan paused, looking up at Solomon's calm face. Then he raised his staff above his head. "Israel from your hand, O king!" he cried. He swung away from them and strode up over the crest of the hill and soon was lost to view, going down upon the left side toward Gibeon.

Solomon took his hand from the mare's bridle, and began to walk his horse, Balkis riding beside him. They came up to the meeting of the roads in silence, and he departed from the road, taking the narrow track along the hill crest. Then she said, "The customs of Israel are very strange to me. In my own land, any who spoke thus to me would be put to death. I have seen Solomon give judgment, and behave as a king should, yet he bowed his head before a ragged and dirty beggar."

"His admonitions may be divinely inspired," said Solomon, gravely. "In any case, such a man acts as the conscience of the king."

"Conscience?" She lifted her eyebrows. "What need has a sovereign of such a commodity? What is right and what is wrong come from the queen who is the flesh of the Goddess—or so it is among us. And that man said that Solomon was not above the law. But is the king himself not the lawgiver? And is not he who gives able also to take away? Is not the giver greater than the gift?"

Solomon said nothing for a time, smoothing absently with one hand the neck of his steed. At last he said, "We do not think that the king is God. I am a man, Balkis, anointed of God. No man can set himself in the place of the Almighty. Our Law is greater than any man for it was the covenant made between our forefathers and Yahweh, when the Lord brought us out of bondage in Egypt and led us through the desert into this land promised us by him. We are the people of his choice, governed by his Law."

"You are a stubborn people," Balkis murmured, "stubborn and conceited. In all the lands where I have journeyed, or all that I ever heard of, the gods of the land permit temples of other gods, and the worship of other gods. But your Yahweh will permit his people none but himself. Jealous is he indeed! All other nations know that their gods are kin to those of other nations, call them by what name you will. Your own temple is built upon the Jebusite altar to Khepa, I am told. And Shapash is the name the Canaanites give to our goddess, Shams, whom the Moabites call Chemosh, worshipping her as a man since, among them, inheritance and rule was through the fathers of tribes. So, too, the Egyptians worship Ra, the Horned Sun;

and their Isis, the Great Mother, is but another name for Babylonian Ishtar and Astarte of the Phoenicians, to whom we also sacrifice as Ashtar, the Lady of the Morning Star. What does your god fear—that he will not receive his full due of burnt meats?"

"Our God neither fears, nor feels pride," said Solomon. "Yet what Balkis says may have a germ of truth in it: that all gods are, indeed, aspects of One. For what is the sun? It is a globe of fire nourishing the world. Like the moon, it is a lamp. It is neither eternal nor unchanging, but was made and set in the heavens—by whom? By One greater than moon or sun or morning star, the maker of all things, the Eternal. He cannot be expressed in an image and yet he is reflected everywhere in his works—in these hills, the blades of grass, the clouds above us, and . . . in us. An image may be carved of the Sun Queen or the Moon King, but how shall we carve an image of the whole world with all its creatures?"

The track led them to the top of a rounded knoll from which they could look out over rolling hills, and valleys in which were silvery-gray olives and dark cypresses. The sun was higher and tiny shimmering waves of heat began to rise from the stony ground. To the north, the knoll fell away in a series of rocky ledges, above which were small grassy spaces where sheep browsed. The gray plume of a shepherd's fire rose from a leafy hollow far below. To the south, a distant twinkling marked the new walls and roofs of the buildings upon Moriah. Solomon dismounted and assisted Balkis from the saddle; they sat down side by side upon a warm, flat stone.

She clasped her hands around her knees, and said, "Well, I will not quarrel further with Solomon. Yet, when I stand before the great image of the Mother in my temple in Marib, I feel her holy strength flow from her benign face into me and I know that I am receiving her power and giving it again to my people. Is this delusion?"

"No, Balkis," he said, turning to her. "The power is the power of the Woman. There are many powers. Here, in my land, many still keep the teraphim in their houses, the wooden images of the household gods. Why do they do so when it is contrary to the word of God? They feel no guilt; it is what has always been done since the earliest times. These crude and humble images are aspects of God, as in a faceted jewel one may see many lights; none are the jewel itself."

He put his hand out upon the rock. A questing ant ran over his finger and stopped, dipping its antennae nervously. He said, "See, now, the humblest of creatures; very marvelous is it to watch them.

I have seen them fight, one against another, and I have watched them run about, full of industry, gathering in provisions in the harvest time against the winter. Have they a king? It may be. Strike into one of their little cities with a dagger and you shall see them rush out, the men with open jaws to defend the citadel, the women bearing their household goods out upon their heads. To them, am I not a god, breaking their temples and houses, visiting punishment upon them for sins too tiny to be perceived?"

He chuckled. "And yet, I am in my turn only one of the works of God, perhaps in my way the least."

She looked at his firm, youthful face with its strong bones and deep eye-hollows, the flash of his white teeth within his beard, and wondered how she could be so content to hear him speak of ants, as he had spoken on other occasions of birds or the ways of beasts with relish and delight, as if these were the most important things in the world. "No," she said, "perhaps not the least, my friend."

He raised his eyes to hers. "I have found many wonders in the earth," he said. "But I have found a greater wonder now. It seems to me I never looked upon a woman before."

He fell silent, looking away, and then he went on, "Once I wrote many songs. I wrote them secretly, and sang them to few people. Songs of praise . . . I was too young to know what to praise. And the past years have been too busy for music. Shall I tell you—?"

"Yes?"

"On that day we first met, a new song came into my heart. Does Balkis remember that I said I had a passing thought which I would tell her one day?"

She did not remember, but she said, "What was it?"

"A phrase, a verse, the beginning of a song. I have been making that song all these days."

"May I hear it?"

"Not yet." He drew away from her, feeling his face grow warm; all his old fear and shyness had come upon him suddenly and he could only think, What if I were to sing it and she laugh at me? What if she thought it inept or trifling or, worse than that, if she should hear all I have declared in this song and it touch her not? "I cannot sing it," he said.

She glanced at him in surprise. Just then, there came an agonized bleating from a little way off; he lifted his head and then stood up.

"A sheep," he said. "Let me look . . ."

She rose and followed him. They saw a ewe that stood near the edge of a cliff; she moved restlessly from side to side, baaing and tossing her head. When they had come closer, they could see that the stony verge had crumbled, and below, caught among bushes that grew out of a crack in the rock, lay a lamb. It had fallen no great distance and was unharmed, but it could not get a footing in the leafy twigs and so it struggled and cried continually in a thin, frightened voice.

Solomon lay down and peered over the edge. Along the face of the cliff ran several long faults. One of these led downward from the edge at an angle; it was perhaps a span wide, and in it were pockets of earth from which grew thick shrubs. At the spot where the lamb was caught, it was no more than eight or nine feet below the edge.

Solomon put off his cloak and his sandals. He went to his horse and unclasped the reins from the bit. He gave the leather strap to Balkis.

"What will you do?" she asked.

"I am going to climb down and get the lamb. Lie down and hold this strap so that I may keep my hand upon it and steady myself."

He began to go along the crack, accordingly, until his head was below the level of the edge of the cliff. Then he took hold of the strap which Balkis held in both her hands. He made his breathing shallow, for the cliff face was almost vertical, and below him was a long drop to the rocky floor of a valley. He shuffled his feet slowly along the crack, stepping on the thick stems of bushes when he could, his left hand gripping the leather reins above his head, his right hand low and extended, palm flat against the rock face. Sweat dripped down from him and wet his bare feet.

When he came to the lamb, he had to brace himself firmly to avoid falling when he lifted it. The creature had ceased its struggles and lay still, only rolling a fearful eye back at him, and now and then uttering a plaintive bleat. He took a better hold on the strap and half turned, wedging one foot into the crack as far as he could, although the skin was torn from his toes in the doing. The other foot he planted upon the fork of a bush, testing it to be sure it would hold. Then, slowly, he bent and seized the lamb by the fleeces of its back.

Balkis, lying flat above him, held her breath. Sharp pebbles dug into her breasts and thighs, and dust was in her nostrils, but she clung grimly to the leather, forgetting that she was a queen, forgetting all her purpose in this land, everything save the terrified lamb and the man below her, who quietly and steadily straightened himself, holding it as one would a puppy. It weighed little so that he could lift it easily, but if it were to struggle the movement might be enough to topple him from his perch. All her world narrowed to this point: the strap, which he held and which united them, his life hanging in her hands.

She saw that he had come nearly upright. The strain on her wrists and fingers was almost intolerable. He bent a trifle, to get the lamb's body against his hip, and slid his arm around the creature to hold it tightly against his body. Then he began to inch backward along the crack.

In a moment or two he had reached a place where he could release the strap and get his arm over the edge of the cliff. Balkis, on her knees now, dropped the strap and caught his wrist with both hands. He swung the lamb up to safety and next instant he was beside her. The lamb scampered to its mother, and Solomon and Balkis were left kneeling, face to face.

"Your garments," he said.

"And you. You are bleeding."

"It is nothing."

A shadow fell across them. "My lord," said a hesitant voice.

They looked up. Half a dozen men, three of Solomon's bodyguard and three of Balkis', stood over them, looking uneasy and frightened. Their spokesman, a squat, flat-nosed Pelethite, gulped once or twice and then repeated, "My lord. Forgive your servant. We saw you on the cliff and hastened . . ."

"From whence have you sprung?" Solomon said, staring. "Out of Sheol? What means this? Did I not command that we be left untroubled?"

"My lord, it was the order of my captain, the son of Abner," said the Pelethite, miserably. "And of the captain of the lady Balkis."

"Arunazel?" Balkis said. "I will have his head." Nevertheless, she began to smile.

"Truly, lady, he would have had our heads if any harm had come to you or to my lord the king. We have followed and watched at a great distance, but when we thought the king in danger—"

Solomon began to laugh, at this. "Very well," he said. "Let us say no more of it. You have done your duty as soldiers. Retire, now, to your distant posts lest your captains punish you, and follow us, for we will return to the city."

The guardsmen saluted and went to their mounts, which they had left a little distance away. Solomon and Balkis also remounted. Before they rode on, however, she brought her mare close to his horse. She leaned forward and put her hand on his.

"I would hear Solomon's song," she said. "Are you so lacking in courtesy that you can deny a guest?"

"Truly, I can deny the queen nothing," he replied.

"Then—come to my garden tonight, when the moon is setting, and sing it to me."

For a moment, he hesitated. He raised her hand to his lips. "Look for me then," he said.

The moon, slanting through the branches of fig and almond trees, dappled the ground with moving silver and cast a sparkle upon the still surface of the cistern. A little owl called softly and sweetly once, and tiny chirps and creaks from among the foliage hardly disturbed the silence of the night.

Like a thief moving among the shadows came the king of Israel. The gate stood a trifle ajar; he entered and closed it behind him. He stood motionless, striving to pierce the confusion of leaf shadows and moonlight. Then, with uncertain steps, he went to the cistern. All was silent.

He had brought his lyre, wrapped in a piece of dark cloth. He drew it out and softly, lest he waken anyone, tuned it. Was she asleep? Had she forgotten? Or had it been a jest, spoken hastily, nothing but mockery? As he waited, he drew the plectrum lightly across the strings, dropping from note to note. He began to hum in accompaniment; then, allowing his verses to fill his mind, he began, very softly, to sing:

> Rise, my love,
>     my beautiful one, come away;
> For see, the winter is past,
>     the rain is over and gone;
> The flowers have appeared on the earth,
>     the time of song has come,
> And the call of the turtle dove
>     is heard in our land;
> The fig tree is putting forth its figs,
>     and the blossoming vines are fragrant.
> Rise, my love,
>     my beautiful one, come away.
> O my dove in the clefts of the rocks
>     in the recesses of the cliffs,

> Let me see your form,
> let me hear your voice;
> For your voice is sweet,
> and your form is comely.

There was a rustle, and from between the fig trees, holding their broad, round leaves away from her face, came Balkis. She passed from the darkness into the light, seeming to float upon the film of her draperies. The low moon shone over her shoulder, through the curve of waist and arm, silvering her dark hair and the pointed tips of her breasts.

Solomon's fingers stilled on the lyre. He sat motionless. All that was lovely in womankind, all that was softness and sweetness came toward him with light steps, on arching feet. Her garments flowed over her thighs like smooth water over stones; her hair was a dark waterfall upon her shoulders. His music was forgotten. He whispered, "Ah, you are beautiful, my love, you are beautiful. Your eyes are doves behind your veil, your hair is like a flock of goats streaming down from Gilead . . . your lips are a thread of scarlet; your two breasts are like two fawns that pasture among the hyacinths . . ."

"I am here," she said. "I have heard. I listened to your voice on the hilltop, I held you when you climbed on the cliffside, I heard your voice singing in the garden and it called me."

He held out his hand to receive hers, to draw her close.

"My dove," he said. "My perfect one."

She came to his arms as a swallow returns to its nest, cleaving to him as one flesh, her lips upon his like honey and milk.

The lyre slipped to the ground, and its strings sounded a single cry, and died away.

# V  THE HORNS OF THE ALTAR

Abishag sat alone upon the rooftop of the palace, a piece of embroidery across her knees. Now and again, she picked listlessly at the threads; she had been sitting here since sunset, and by now it was too dark to work, yet she remained, unable to move, her thoughts treading a weary, familiar round like an ox harnessed to the olive press. The king, she thought, the king and the woman of Sheba.

Yet it was not so much jealousy that nagged at her as the sense of loss: in this brief time she had been robbed of all that made life bearable, for the king never came nowadays to the rooftop to talk with her. She, who had neither husband nor child, loved hopelessly; like a beggar, she had been content with crumbs, with the friendship of Solomon, with the role of sister and confidante since she could have nothing more. Not even that was left her now.

It was common knowledge in the king's household that Solomon went every night to the house of Balkis, that he crept thither in darkness, fancying himself unobserved and secret (yet how can the doings of a king remain secret long?) and that he remained with her until daybreak. The God of Israel was a god of men; in silence and mystery the women still spoke the ancient charms for childbirth and love, still kept by them the crude images of the Canaanite or Philistine goddess with the swollen belly and her accompanying doves, or serpents, still spoke their inmost prayers to her to ease the pains of birth, or the issue of blood which each month she visited upon them. What did Yahweh know of such things? He had made Israel great among the nations, but his love was reserved for his sons; he was a god of warriors and priests, and even to enter the holy part of his Temple or to take part in what was done there was forbidden to women. How could Solomon thus know the power of the Sheban goddess? He could never understand, as Abishag clearly understood, the nature of his enmeshment. He was like some noble stag leaping from his covert to be tangled in the hunters' nets: he does not understand what it is that holds him, but strikes with his hoofs, shakes his great antlers, threatens the unseen and unknown foe and falls, at last, helpless before the spear. For Solomon, Balkis would be no more than a woman, but Abishag knew well that she was much more than that—she was, when she chose to be, the Goddess herself, the oldest and strongest enemy of Yahweh.

Then the shaft of jealousy pierced her as she thought of the king in the arms of Balkis. A whole host of memories arose: she remembered the night he had known her, here, upon this very couch, with a tenderness and urgency which she had mistaken for love. How she had deluded herself, and how cruel that next morning when he had stared coldly at her as if without recognition. Mine once, if only that once, she said to herself, and fancied him clasping Balkis close, kissing and caressing her, undoing her girdle and knowing her body . . .

She had thought herself free of jealousy because each time Solomon had taken a wife she had felt nothing of this, no pang. But that was deception, for he had had no love for either Tuosri or Mahalath: they were marriages of state and of convenience. She had been able to tell herself that it was she who held his heart, she to whom he turned for all but the brief solace of the couch. It was a lie! She had never had him, even for an instant; he had waited all this time for Balkis as if knowing she would some day appear, as it was written, "Bone of my bone, flesh of my flesh . . . thus it is that a man leaves both father and mother and clings to his beloved."

She rose in torment, casting the embroidery aside, and walked to the low parapet. She gazed over, into the murk below, at the fringed shadows of trees through which her body could hurtle without hindrance; one dreadful rush, one instant of agony and all would be finished. Her father and her brothers would weep for her—but Solomon would not weep.

She tore herself from the vision of her death, and went toward the stair. Sittar had been sitting quietly on the parapet near the stairhead, watching her; he stood up and said, "Maiden."

She almost cried out, for she had not noticed him in the gloom nor heard him come.

"Do not be frightened," he said hastily.

"What do you want?" she demanded, indignant at being spied on, as she thought.

Sittar approached a few steps. "I did not know anyone was here. I came for a breath of air."

"And having seen that someone *was* here—?"

"By the face of Ilmuqa," he said, humbly, "I am a liar. I knew Abishag was here; if she had not been, the rooftop would have been barren as a wilderness. I came only to look at you, to speak with you if it is permitted."

She could not control a smile. And having once smiled, she said, "Who am I to give or withhold permission to the prince of Sheba? Let him speak, if he will."

Sittar scratched his head and looked helplessly at the starry sky. "Good enough. Now that I may speak, I can think of nothing to say."

"Then I will leave you."

"Do not go!" he said quickly. "How can Abishag be so cruel? Is it the way of Israelite maidens to crush men beneath their heels, to tread on them as if they were worms?"

She laughed at his extravagance, and he laughed with her. "Well," he said, "I have cheered you a little. I have watched Abishag these past few days, and I have seen her face fill with sadness. Always she sits with downcast eyes, like one who has lost a friend."

"Wherein is it your affair?"

"You are right. It might be none of my affair—save that my sister is involved in it, as well as my friend Solomon."

"Ah," she said, at that, "your sister . . ."

"Now may I speak? Let Abishag believe I mean her only good." He spoke rapidly, earnestly, as if afraid she might leave him before he could finish. "You have not lost Solomon, he is your friend still. But I would be more than a friend. You and I should comfort each other, for Solomon sees me no more, nor has he time for me. Can we not help each other forget—"

He tried to touch her, but she stepped away, saying bitterly, "Oh, you Shebans are all love-mad. While the sister ensnares the son of David, the brother would console himself with the king's hand-maiden."

He stopped. "It is not so," he said, in a choking voice. "By my life, I swear it. You are neither Solomon's wife nor concubine, nor his handmaiden. If you were dear to him I would say nothing, for he is my friend and my brother. But from the moment I first saw Abishag in the lamplight upon this rooftop I have hungered for her. By Shams who made me, I can neither eat nor sleep—"

He fell silent. Then, looking into her face, he said in an altered voice, "You love him."

She nodded.

"Ah," he said, "you love him and he knows it not?"

"He knows nothing of it," she answered. "Sittar is very kind. I wish only that I might give my heart to him."

"Kind," he repeated. Then he sighed. "It has been said of me that I am light-minded. But may the arrow of Ilmuqa smite me if I ever change in this. Remember, I am here. Whenever Abishag feels sorrow, let her turn to me." He took her hand and this time she did not resist, but allowed him to kiss it. Then he said, "Shall I go or stay?"

She hesitated. At last she said, "Stay, if it pleases you. But sit further off, on the parapet yonder, and I will sit upon the couch."

It did her good to have him there, and now that the barrier had been broken between them and all confessed and in the open, she could talk freely. She had not realized how much she needed this: to have someone to whom she could pour out her heart, to whom she could tell her woes, her loneliness, her unrequited love. And Sittar listened and sympathized, spoke little of himself, then came to joke, and by degrees raised her spirits so that she laughed, who had never thought to laugh again.

It was thus Solomon found them, a little after the rise of the moon when he came to the rooftop. Balkis could not see him this night for there had come, late in the afternoon, letters and reports from Sheba, sent northward by a spice caravan, which required her attention. Accordingly, the king had turned to the many petitions and accounts of his own which had accumulated, unlooked at, during the past week, and had spent several intensive hours with his scribe disposing of them. Then, finding himself restless and unable to sleep, he had gone roaming through the palace to find his way at last to the roof, when he heard the low voices and laughter.

He said, while yet on the stairhead, "Will it please my friends to let me come and join them for a little while?"

"My lord Solomon may command his servants as he pleases," said Abishag.

"No, no. That is unkind." He sounded hurt. "If I must command—"

Sittar jumped up and went to him at once. "Then it is I who will command," he said, gripping his friend's arm. "Come up and sit with us."

"But if Abishag will not have it—"

"Nothing would more delight me," she said. "It was only that I did not look to see Solomon here, and I was taken by surprise."

"That is true," said Sittar, settling himself on the parapet beside Solomon. "We have seen little of my friend for many days. We know well the affairs of state that occupy his mind—"

"Do not jest," Solomon said. "There need be no deception between me and my cousin. His sister has taken my heart in her hands."

Sittar ran his fingers through his hair, and stretched. "Oh," he said, "did I not tell my cousin once that all who met her loved her? I have seen iron out of the sky which draws other iron to it; she has that power over men."

"Still, you do not understand." Solomon clasped his hands tightly between his knees. "How can I make my cousin see that this is no idle fancy? She is more to me than my kingdom."

Sittar grinned. "Is my cousin happy?"

"Happier than ever in my life before." He had been sitting hunched forward, and now he straightened, looking directly into Sittar's face. "I can see that Sittar refuses to believe me. What, then, would you say if I were to tell you that it is in my mind to wed the daughter of Merisamis?"

"To wed her?" It burst from both Abishag and Sittar almost simultaneously.

Solomon looked from one to the other. "Does this surprise you?"

They were silent, their faces pale under the waning moon, turned toward him like those of ghosts.

"Does this not please you?" he said. And, as they still remained silent, he went on, in a tone of annoyance, "Can you not speak? Why should we not wed if we love one another?"

"My lord," Abishag said, at length, "it may not be." Objections of all sorts sprang into her mind, but she was too startled and confused to voice them.

However, Sittar said, "She is right. What could give me greater joy than to have Solomon for my brother? Yet surely he must see that the God of Israel cannot take the Threefold One as his bride. The succession to the throne would be ever in dispute. How would the two lands be governed? Which would rule? There are too many problems—"

Solomon stood up. Those first unfortunate words of Abishag's when he had come up on the roof had wounded him more than he thought, and he had felt shut out of their intimacy. Now it seemed to him that they were resolved to be cold to him, to turn him away as they had attempted to do when first he arrived. "I see well," he said, frigidly, "that problems come more readily to your lips than good wishes. Do not imagine I cannot see what is in your minds, both of you—you are too jealous of my friendship and it pains you to think I might turn from you and love another. Is that not so?"

"It is false!" Sittar cried. "Solomon, Solomon, what has come upon you? We think only of you—"

"You think of yourselves," he said, in the same harsh, distant tone. "I came expecting to find true friends, allies in my happiness, ready to share with me. But put the flawed blade to the test and it breaks. Go, then; let Abishag and Sittar turn to each other and laugh, and speak softly in the dark. I need them not. Tomorrow I will take counsel in this matter. If I must stand alone, I will do so. Only beware; do not think to come between me and my desire."

He left them. Abishag started toward the stair, but Sittar caught her arm.

"Do not follow him," he said.

"But he must not think evil of us!"

"It was not Solomon who spoke," Sittar said, shaking his head. "It was a demon of madness."

"Madness?" She put a hand to her throat.

"I do not doubt of it," said the prince. "He is a man mad with love. Ashtar has touched him. May his God Yahweh protect him now, for there is nothing we can do."

On the morrow, the king brought together his counselors, who included, besides Benaiah the commander of the host, Zadok the high priest, and Jehoshaphat the recorder, Chimham the son of Barzillai, Azariah the son of Zadok, Elihoreph the chief scribe, Shimei the son of Ela, a Benjamite; and in addition, the commander of the garrisons, the chief of all his governors, the officer in charge of forced labor; Joel the son of Abner, who commanded his bodyguard; and Ahushai the son of Asaph, who was the king's steward—so that there were twelve of them in all. Rarely did Solomon consult them all at once, save on matters of great importance, preferring to allow each to deal within his own province with his own affairs, and taking counsel on matters of state with the three elders: Chimham, Azariah, and Shimei. Therefore, there was a great deal of soft-voiced speculation and whispering as they waited for the king, sitting about the long table which had been placed in the throne room, and nibbling fruit and nuts or drinking the light, thin, morning wine.

Solomon entered at last, and gravely took his seat at the head of the table. He had gone, very early, to the Temple, where before the Holy of Holies he had prostrated himself, praying for guidance and yet fearful to hear the voice of his God. He already repented deeply of his anger against Sittar and Abishag, but he said nothing to either of them, not only for shame but because he dreaded lest anything weaken his resolve. He knew all too well the obstacles against marriage with Balkis, but he could no more draw back than can a man who has leaped over a cliff. All things faded before the force of his love: his friends, his counselors, his kingship. And even the power of the Lord was not sufficient to divert him from his course, for even as he lay upon his face whispering, "King over the Universe, give me your blessing," his mind strayed: he was in the garden with Balkis, hearing her voice, not that of God. In the end, weary and unanswered, he had risen and gone out of the Temple, his mind in confusion, and within his breast a strange, hollow feeling of unrest and dissatisfaction.

He looked about at the faces of his counselors, all intent and, it seemed to him, full of accusation. Thus he felt himself at once on the defensive, and he began to speak in a sharper tone than he had wished to use.

"We have come together," he said, "to discuss a matter of the greatest importance to the future of Israel. Heretofore, when I have taken a wife, I have not found it expedient or necessary to debate the question with any save the three elder of you. But now . . ."

He paused, for at the words "taken a wife," the atmosphere became heavy with tension, and he saw the looks that passed between some of them.

"I know," he said, beginning to bristle, although he strove to keep himself calm, "that many objections will come to your minds. Nevertheless, let us consider the matter without passion. It is my thought to take Balkis the queen of Sheba for my wife."

He could have secured no more violent effect if he had bidden them eat unclean food. Elihoreph dropped with a clatter the waxed tablet on which he was making notes; Benaiah and Joel stared at each other unhappily but silently; the others were glaring at him or muttering together. He leaned back in his chair, folding his arms.

The son of Barzillai said, in a quavering voice, "My lord King Solomon, may I speak?"

"Say on."

The old man clenched his pale and shaking fingers in his snowy beard. "Surely the king has considered all the problems that would arise. If this—if the queen were to have a son, would he rule over Israel and Sheba? Nor might the queen enter Solomon's household, being queen over her own country. Would she, therefore, sit upon the throne of judgment beside our lord the king? And what if—may

Yahweh avert the evil chance—our lord should die? Would Israel be ruled by a woman? Surely, as I say, our lord Solomon must have considered all these things. Let him, therefore, tell us his own conclusions so that we may benefit from his wisdom."

"All these points which the son of Barzillai has mentioned," said Solomon, glowering, "are trivial. The queen rules her own land, and I rule mine. If we should wed, it would unite Sheba with Israel by a bond stronger than any other. As for her son, if she have one, he will not succeed to the throne of David."

He was conscious, as he spoke, that he had not really answered all the arguments but he could not think clearly; a cloud lay upon his mind, of defeat foreordained. If only Balkis were beside him, he thought, to give him strength with her smile and her love.

Meanwhile, Shimei the son of Ela, was saying, "—and if it were so, that the king ousts him from the succession, then we should have bloody war. For see, Absalom the son of Maacah went not to his grandfather's country, the kingdom of Geshur, to be king there, but remained in Israel and rose up against his father, David, seeking to secure the throne. And what if such a son should come against us with all the might of Sheba, to enforce his claims?"

"The son of Ela speaks as if there were already such a son," Benaiah put in. "It may be they will have nothing but daughters . . ."

He smiled, in a conciliatory fashion, hoping to lighten the air, but it was useless.

Zadok, sitting stiffly in his chair, said in a loud voice, "Such a marriage would bring nothing but disaster upon Israel. If she were not a queen . . . But in this case, be certain that the sword of revolt will be raised. Have you forgotten the son of Bichri, the Benjamite, who in the days of Absalom's rebellion cried, 'We have no portion in the son of Jesse—to your tents, O Israel!'? Speak, Shimei. Will Benjamin follow the king in this marriage? Or will they return to their tents?"

"Alas, my lord, I fear they will not follow," said Shimei, shaking his head.

"Judah will stand by the king," snapped Joel, "even as it was before, for he is of our kin. Let the others withdraw. Let it be sung of them as it was of Reuben in the days of Barak, 'Why did you lounge among the ravines while your brothers exposed themselves to death?'"

Zadok looked at the king with a grim and level gaze. "There, my lord king, behold the result," he said. "Already there is dissension. And the tribes will divide even as your council is divided."

Chimham put in, "There is one thing which may decide the issue for us. Let our lord the king say whether Yahweh is with him. For he passed the early hours of the day before the Holy of Holies. Speak, my lord, and tell us: what says the voice of God?"

Solomon sat back, looking blackly upon these men who soured his joy and sullied his love. "Am I the king—?" he said, thickly.

"Truly, my lord, you are the king," said the recorder, Jehoshaphat, in a mild and bleating voice. "And it is for you to speak the word that will resolve us. God forbid we should do other than advise."

"But consider," said Zadok, raising an admonitory finger in the air. "Will the king bring dismay and death to Israel and Judah? Or did he not swear to bring peace to our land?"

At the word "peace," Solomon's anger began to evaporate. He drew a deep breath, and said more quietly, "Well, I have listened. Long ago, even as Zadok says, I swore that in my reign I would bring peace to Israel and make her secure among the nations. This work I have accomplished. I will do nothing willfully to break that peace. Yet remember that of two ways to choose there is always a third. Let me weigh all these points and try if I may find some surety for you that will satisfy all doubts. The council is ended."

They all rose up and left him, some swiftly, some hesitantly. A long time he sat there alone, turning and twisting a reed pen between his fingers. He had acted, up to now, as a man driven by lust alone. But at this moment, seeing clearly the opposition of all, he knew certainly and without doubt that he loved Balkis, that she was indeed dearer to him than life itself, and that he would not give her up without a struggle.

He took a sheet of papyrus, dipped the pen in the bowl of ink that stood beside his hand, and wrote, "From the king of Judah and Israel . . ."

He looked at the words for a long time, and then slowly crossed them out. He wrote, "Hatred stirs up strife; but love draws a veil over all transgressions."

Then, with a sigh, he pushed back his chair and got up. Zabud had been sitting on the floor in a corner, dozing lightly; at Solomon's touch upon his shoulder he woke at once and sprang to his feet.

"Go," said the king, "and find the queen of Sheba, and say to her that I cannot see her for today or tomorrow, for I have much to ponder—affairs of state that may not be denied. Ask her to forgive me, and say that I will come to her again when I can."

In his house at Bethlehem, Joab the son of Zeruiah was preparing for the journey south, to the city of Tamar where he would take up the command of the garrison. In an evil humor he poked through the heap of armor and weapons which his armor-bearer Gareb had brought for his inspection, kicking aside with his foot those pieces which needed repair or were too worn to take. Here was a bronze sword he had worn thirty years before in the wars against the Philistines. At the siege of Gath it had been bent almost double by the blow of a club, and in being straightened it had cracked. He had put it aside after that battle, meaning to have it reforged, but it had been forgotten. Yet all these years it had gone with him from place to place for the sake of its hilt, which was of silver. Useless lumber! like sentiment, like love, like friendship, which men carried with them for small cause, unable to rid themselves of it but profiting nothing by it. "Throw it away," he growled to Gareb. "And this, too, this rusty helmet which was given me by David once. Why should I keep it longer? David is dead, and I also am dead. Let me at least go to the grave in decent clothing."

He strode to the window, for the rattle of a chariot and the thudding of hoofs had come to his ears. Leaning his forehead against the cool bronze bars, he saw Adonijah rein in just outside with such violence that his horses were thrown against the chariot tongue. Four or five armed horsemen were with him, among them Nebat the Ephraimite in a leather coat and kirtle. The prince tossed the reins to his armor-bearer and jumped from the chariot. In a moment or two he was brought in to Joab.

"How like a bridegroom looks the son of Haggith," said Joab, mockingly. "Have you come to bid me feast at your wedding?"

Adonijah glared at him. "Let the son of Zeruiah be grateful for his age, or I would break him between my hands like a stick," he said.

"Oh, you are bold to me. Save your boldness for the king. You nicely botched it between you, you and Bathsheba. Why would you not listen to me, and begin slowly? Why could you not keep out of sight until Bathsheba had prepared the ground?"

"Enough!" Adonijah roared. "We have trodden that ground a hundred times. We are like to have another sort of wedding feast if we do not act quickly."

Joab regarded him with a frown. Then he sat down on a chest under the window. "Well, speak," he said.

Adonijah hooked his thumbs in his girdle. "You know that Azariah the son of Nathan, who commands the king's garrisons, has long been a friend of mine. This morning, he brought me word that the king has announced to his counselors that he intends to marry the Sheban queen."

Joab raised an eyebrow. "Go on."

"They opposed it. He ended by saying that he would yet find a way to do so."

"No doubt the son of Haggith sees a hidden significance in the matter. The king has taken wives before. If he takes this one, it will the sooner bring his throne crashing down."

Adonijah smote his hands together. "But this may be the moment I have waited for—the moment she promised me. 'I will make him blind and unwary,' she said."

Joab sighed, holding up his hand. "I do not know who this 'she' is. Indeed, Solomon is sometimes wise, and he has said, 'The mouth of a fool precipitates ruin.' Begin, therefore, at the beginning."

Therewith, mastering his irritation at the old man's insults, Adonijah told how Balkis had met with him in the garden and of the bargain they had made. When he had finished, Joab sat for a while staring at the floor and tapping his finger tips together. At length, he said, "And now?"

"Why, by my hand," said Adonijah, "is not this the very moment to strike? He brings down destruction upon his head. Let us go up against him with every man. Besides—"

"Besides, Adonijah would have the woman in his bed, and speedily," Joab put in, drily. "Is that not it?"

"And if it were?"

"Then it blinds you. The time is not yet ripe."

"Wherefore not, in God's name?"

"Listen, son of Haggith. I am old and wise in the ways of war, if nothing else. I bear more scars upon my body than other men have hairs. The time to fall upon the enemy is not when he is strong, but when he is weak, not after he has risen from sleep and eaten and refreshed himself, but when he has gone to his rest, or early in the morning before he has awakened. Now the king is still strong. Not yet is it known what the council debated, nor has he made public his desire to marry Balkis. If that time should come, the tribes will divide against him or for him. Then is the moment to strike, not before. To act prematurely might only unite them against us. As for the Sheban woman—how know you she is not a double-dealer with you, as she is with Solomon? To trust a woman is like seizing oil with one's hand. How if her tale of Hadad and his armies be a lie, and the only armies waiting in the desert be Sheban ones, ready to seize all for their queen?"

Adonijah was silent, but a frown as dark as a thundercloud gathered on his brows. He turned toward the door.

"Where are you going?" Joab asked.

"To Jerusalem. I will take the woman by the throat and see if I may not wring the truth from her."

"Wait. There is another possibility."

"Speak."

"You say this amulet of hers is the signal for the Edomite to attack?"

"So she said."

"If we could secure this amulet," Joab murmured. "If I might have it in my hand when I go down to Tamar, then I could see for myself whether Hadad is in truth there with his host. And if so—why should we not make our own bargain with him?"

"With Hadad?" Adonijah's lip lifted. "You are to him a name to curse by."

"Hm . . . Sometimes a man will ally himself with the wolf against the viper, choosing the lesser of two evils. Have we a man we can trust, to steal the pendant for us?"

Adonijah nodded. "It may be so. There is a dwarf in the queen's service, a certain Haran, who swore to help me if I would get him his freedom."

"Good." Joab arose, and placed a hand on the prince's shoulder. "If it may be done, do it, and send the amulet here to me as quick as may be. If I have gone, I will leave a servant to carry it for me."

Adonijah seized the hand on his shoulder in a grip of iron. "I will do it," he said, menacingly. "Only, let Joab remember that it is I who command. It seems to me the son of Zeruiah sometimes forgets himself."

Joab's eyes did not waver. Disengaging his hand, he said, "If my words are sometimes rude, it is because I am a soldier, not a gallant. Yet I have called myself the servant of Adonijah. Was I not the first to hail him king? Was it not on his behalf that I risked exile? It is not for myself I work, but for my lord's welfare. Therefore, when my lord is king let him forgive his servant."

Adonijah nodded. "When I am king," he said, "it shall be forgiven."

When the prince came out of the house, Nebat the Ephraimite came forward and said, motioning to one of the horsemen, "My cousin, take the horse of Bani, here, and ride beside me, for I have something to say to you."

Adonijah grunted. Without comment, he let the soldier get into the chariot, and himself mounted the man's steed. He and Nebat rode out ahead of the others.

Nebat said, "My cousin knows I have great respect for the son of Zeruiah."

"I, too. Yet there may come a day, very soon, when I must show him which of us two is master and which servant."

"Is it not said that the beauty of an old man is his gray hair? It seems to me that he who was once commander of the host has grown overcautious with age."

"Overcautious?"

" 'The time to fall upon the enemy is not when he is strong, but when he is weak,' " Nebat quoted, grinning. "Oh, my cousin need not look so surprised. In his interest, I listened beneath the window."

"The son of Ahijah presumes on his friendship with me," Adonijah began, coldly.

Instead of answering, Nebat caught the bridle of the prince's horse and pulled him to a halt. Turning in the saddle, he motioned the men behind to stop at a distance. In a low voice, he said to Adonijah, "My cousin, listen to me. I do not presume. Of all those who pretend friendship with Adonijah, whom can he better trust than myself? Have we not sworn oaths of brotherhood?"

His eyes glowed, and his voice shook with the fervency of his emotion. "By my hand," he said, "Adonijah is dearer to me than my father, dearer than my wife. I have gone beside him to En-rogel, and followed him ever since, for love of him. My blood is his. May God do so to me and more if I lie."

Adonijah regarded him somberly. "You do not lie. Say on."

"I do not fear a strong enemy. Neither did Joab when he was younger. But now—why should we wait for that old spider to spin his webs? Let us strike now, even as my cousin wished. But not with soldiers—no, for then it would be said we rebelled. If the king should die . . ."

"Die?"

"Just so. If he should die, would not all Israel hail Adonijah? Who else may rule? Would not the council sigh with relief at this resolving of their difficulties? From them to the Elders of the tribes is but a step. And when the full tale is known, all Israel will bless the hand that delivered them from marriage with Sheba."

Adonijah chewed his lip. To rise up against his brother with armed men, to fight openly, sword in hand, this was all within his nature. What Nebat suggested awoke in him a repulsion hard to put a name to: it was no longer simply a question of his right to the throne, but a matter of the death of his brother—and of the king. Ancient and powerful was the curse placed on any who lifted a hand against the Lord's anointed. And more ancient yet the punishment against the man who slew his brother. Fear and desire warred within him; he could neither refuse the temptation nor accept it. At last, he said, "It is too much. What man would do such a thing?"

Nebat's lips tightened. "Let me contrive it," he said. "There are matters to which a king's son need not put his hand, but say only 'yea' to his servants, to fetch or carry for him. Let my cousin continue as he and Joab have planned. Only, it may be I can hasten events for him."

Adonijah looked into the dark, passionate face with its full, womanish lips and burning eyes. He could not bear the fire in it, and turned away his head. In a muffled voice he said, "Let my cousin do as he wishes. I give my assent."

At the same time, an uncontrollable shudder seized him. He clapped heels to his horse and began to gallop, as if he could escape from his own decision by speed.

Balkis awoke slowly when the first ray of the sun touched her eyelids. She stretched languorously, running her hand over her breast and side; she cast aside the coverlet, and with her left arm under her head she looked sleepily at her body. She took pleasure in its perfection, as if it were not hers, admiring the smoothness of her skin, now golden where the sun shone on it, now tawny in shadow. She stroked the firm curve of her thigh and closed her eyes; unbidden, the thought of Solomon entered her mind, as it had more and more frequently during the past two days of his absence.

Ah, he was ardent! In all his ways there was the furious love of life, nothing between, nothing lukewarm. That he loved her she knew, but there were times when the intensity of his desire almost frightened her: his body burned, and the touch of his hand awakened in her an answering flame that consumed all sense and devoured the coolness of her will. And he was changeable to meet her changes, quick to move with her mood: now gentle and full of mild endearments, now like a leopard biting her throat and rending her flesh.

She turned her head restlessly to shut out the thought of him and sat up in bed, taking her face between her hands. Was this not what she had aimed for, to madden him and bend him to her wish? Now he was hers, and there remained only to summon Hadad, to play upon Adonijah's greed and weakness, to hurl them all three together and let them tear each other to pieces. To consider her cleverness and her coming victory restored her sense of self; was she not the personification of Shams, the Threefold One, maid, wife, and mother, superior to any man, receiving but not giving save of her own volition, and never permanently?

She leaped from her bed naked as she was, and walked restlessly about the room. She had been too hot; now she was chilled, and snatched up the coverlet and wrapped it about herself. Something strange and terrible was happening to her, to which she could give no name, but where once she had felt alone in the security of her divinity and her rule, she now felt close beside her an intruder, another soul that pressed upon her own, clamorous and not to be denied.

She swung round, folding the coverlet close about her as if to escape—from whom? from what?—and went with quick, uneven steps to a little bell that hung beside the bed; she struck it to summon her handmaidens, hoping by their chatter and activity to abolish the haunting presence.

When they came trooping in, one of them said, "Lady, there is a messenger waiting below with word from the king of Israel."

"What word?" she said, almost shrilly. He had emerged, then, from his silence, from the work which must have absorbed him, the "affairs of state" of which his last message had spoken.

"The king bid him say that if the queen desired it, he wished to ride out with her today."

The blood rushed to her face. In an instant, she had thrust away all the uncertainties and hesitations that had beset her. She said, "Go, one of you, and say to the messenger that it *is* the queen's desire. The rest, come and attire me at once."

When she had dressed, she hastily broke her fast with milk, dates and cheese. She was just finishing when one of her servants came to say that the king had just ridden up before the house. She took up a hooded cloak and went to join him.

He seemed moody and abstracted this morning, and although he greeted her courteously there was lacking the warmth she had come to expect. As a result, she herself became more reserved. Nor was he alone, for there were with him his own armor-bearer, Zabud, and six guardsmen, as well as three lead horses with bundles slung across their saddles.

He said, "A blessed morning on which I once again behold the queen. I have prepared for a journey to the forest of Ephraim. Is this agreeable to you?"

"Whatever is your will is mine also," she replied, distantly.

He glanced sharply at her, and with a dark shadow in his eyes.

He said nothing, however, but assisted her to mount. They rode off together, the troop following.

By midday they had come by way of Jericho into the wide plain of the Jordan where, on the eastern foothills of the mountains, a thick forest began. Here, in a grassy glade not far from a stream, they made a camp: tents were unpacked and set up, a cloth spread, and provisions prepared for the noonday meal. They ate as they had ridden, mostly in silence, and when they were done the king said, "Zabud, remain here with the soldiers. All of you may sleep, now that the sun is high. But if the queen will, she may come with me, for I have something to show her."

They walked together under the spreading branches, following an almost indistinguishable path which led upward over a shoulder of the hill and down again into a fan-shaped valley where the trees were larger and stood further apart. At the head of the valley the ground rose sharply to a great, outthrust precipice of limestone, rounded at the top like a brooding head above them. Below, where the valley widened to the plain, the forest marched almost to the banks of the winding river. Solomon led her to a grove of oaks just below the massive rock cliff. The trees had been cut away within the grove to make a wide, circular space, and here there was a cairn of stones twice the height of a man.

"This is the grave of my brother, Absalom," he said.

She looked upon it with distaste, shuddering, for gloomy and wild was the air of this place. The valley was silent as if neither bird nor beast dwelt in it. Only as they stood, they heard a hollow clattering of pebbles falling somewhere, and then the silence closed in again.

"Why have you brought me here?" she said. "Little joy does there seem in the day now. Indeed, I would have been happier had I remained in Jerusalem. In two days I have not seen Solomon, and now—"

He sighed, and took her hand. He drew her to sit beside him on the rough trunk of a fallen oak, and still holding her hand he said, "Forgive me, Balkis, for there is a sorrow upon me. In this place, Absalom was buried; in this wood he lost his life. He was very handsome, very proud and fair, beloved by all who knew him. But his desire was to be king over the land, and in the vehemence of his desire he forgot the Law: Honor your father and your mother. Remember that I once told you the Law was above all men. Absalom forgot all things—he was heedless and impetuous, and led by evil counsel so that he drew about him the men of Israel and proclaimed himself king in Hebron. He would have slain our father, David, and

only the power of God prevented him from doing so. For the armies
of Absalom, and the men of Judah and others who were loyal to my
father, met in this forest and there was a great battle. Twenty thousand were here slain, and as Absalom was riding upon his mule he
was caught in the branches of an oak and held fast. And there Joab
came upon him, and in spite of the word of my father that none
should harm my brother, Joab stabbed him through with a dart and
slew him."

"It is a gloomy tale," said Balkis. "Was it to cheer my heart you
told it me?"

"No, no," said Solomon. "I brought you here and told you this story
that you might better understand the dreadful choice I have to
make, I, myself. Help me, Balkis!"

He clenched his hand suddenly upon hers with such force that her
rings were driven into her fingers and she cried out with pain. He
released her, and drew a little away and she could see the torment
upon his face.

"What is it?" she said, now gentle. "Speak."

He said, "On the day before yesterday, I went in to my council
and told them I desired to wed the queen of Sheba."

Her eyes widened. She stared at him, transfixed and speechless.

"It is so," he said. "I had, first, to see what my counselors would say
to this before I spoke of it with you. It was made plain to me that if
I persisted in such a course many of my own people would turn
against me. Listen—when my father named me to be king after him,
I was filled with elation, for I had long since hoped that I might some
day bring peace to Israel. I have done so, in despite of all. That lies
upon the one hand. But now, on the other, lies what I never considered, a new thing: my love for you."

Still she stared at him, her mind divided, one part of her tri-
umphant, the other numb and uncomprehending.

"My love for you," he repeated, almost with a sob. "I have an
Absalom within me, ready to do battle with me for his desire, un-
caring of what ruin it may bring. I would to God I might lay him
beneath such a heavy cairn of stones as this."

She said, in a whisper, "Solomon—"

He covered her hands with his. "My bride," he said. "My beloved.
How shall I say it to you? Is there no way, my God?"

He bowed his head forward and kissed her hands. And on his
motion, something hissed through the air over his bent back and
struck with a thump in the earth behind him.

With his next breath, knowing the thing for what it was, he hurled his weight against Balkis, pushing her backward from their seat. He fell upon her, huddling her close to the ground on the other side of the fallen tree. A second javelin rushed over them and clanged against a hidden stone.

"Lie still!" he said to Balkis. He moved cautiously, squirming round to peer over the tree trunk. The sun fell between the columns of trees, and the gently moving leaves cast deceptive shadows beneath.

A voice, low but distinct in the silence, said, "Too late. Quick, before he cries out—"

Four men burst from among the trees, running with drawn swords in their hands. The foremost vaulted a boulder at the edge of the cairn; his lips were drawn back in a mirthless grin like a wolf's and the whites of his eyes flashed in his brown face.

Solomon sprang to his feet. He plucked from the ground the first javelin. He had barely time to reverse it when the assassin was upon him. Too late, the man saw the brown iron and strove to halt or turn aside. Solomon lunged with the weapon in both hands. He felt the shock of meeting in his wrists, the heavy weight against his arms; he was almost face to face with his antagonist when blood burst from the other's mouth and soaked the king's tunic.

A blade shone high above him. He heard a muffled curse and felt someone push him from behind. He fell with the body of his assailant beneath him.

The hilt of a sword, slippery with blood, was under his clutching hand. He took hold of it and dragged himself to his knees.

An unearthly screeching filled the grove. He caught a glimpse of Balkis with her arm drawn back, and realized that she must have found the other spear. Even with the thought he saw her cast it. He did not see where it went. A man ran past him. Solomon staggered erect and threw the sword underhand with all his strength; he saw the blade streak through the air and bury itself in the man's body. The fellow gave a leap like a stag and fell heavily on his face, twisting and drumming with his feet against the earth.

He heard galloping, and between the trees he saw a horseman riding away toward the river.

"One escaped," said a familiar voice. He turned to see Zabud, pale as whey, blood welling slowly from a deep slash in his shoulder. The armor-bearer smiled faintly and slumped down. "Forgive . . ." he said. ". . . cannot stand."

Balkis, her hands shaking, was already tearing a strip of cloth from her tunic. It was not for Zabud, however, but for Solomon; she was staring at the blood which clotted the front of his tunic.

"I am unhurt," he said. He took the cloth from her and went to Zabud. Gently, he bound the cloth over the wound and drew it as tight as he dared, to stop the bleeding.

As he did so, Zabud said weakly, "I could not remain behind . . . Once before, my lord said 'Sleep,' and when I did so, the lion . . . So I followed. Forgive my disobedience."

"Be quiet, Zabud," said Solomon. "God led you to my aid. It is a deep wound but it will heal. Do not move; be still, and rest."

He turned to Balkis. She was leaning back against a tree and he could see the sweat glisten on her face. Abruptly, she turned her head away from him and was sick.

He put his arm about her, supporting her, and helped her to sit down upon the ground. "Brave heart," he said.

"Alas, alas, it is a heavy thing to slay a man," she murmured. "I saw Zabud run out and thought him one of them. He pushed you down just as the second man raised his sword. He took the blow upon his shoulder, and stabbed the man in the belly. The man fled, bending and holding his bowels, and I—"

"Enough," said Solomon. "Do not think of it." Tenderly, he wiped her face with the hem of his tunic. Then he left her and went to look at the dead.

The first man who had come at him was lying on his face, doubled up, the javelin's head emerging from between his shoulder blades. Solomon turned him over and looked into the face of Nebat the Ephraimite. The other two he did not know. He stood for a long time, staring down into the dark, handsome face, twisted with the rage and anguish of death. Then he swung round abruptly.

"I must return to Jerusalem," he said. "At once. Can you walk, Zabud? I dare not leave you lest that one who escaped should come again with others."

"I can walk," said the armor-bearer. "If my lord will but let me hold his arm."

They made what speed they could up the path, but they had not gone above a hundred paces when they met the six guardsmen running down toward them. Solomon left four of them with Zabud and the queen, ordering them to strike the camp and follow him when they could. Zabud, he commanded them to bring to a physician in Jericho. With the other two guards, he hastened to the horses; he sprang into the saddle and sped away like the wind upon the Jerusalem road.

Much as he loved horses, he did not spare his steed but drove it on mercilessly, and entered the city before dusk. The guardsmen were far behind him. He slipped from his mount at the gates and told the startled watchman to see that the trembling beast was cared for. He went on foot, dusty and bloodstained as he was, to the barracks of his bodyguard. His mind was red with anger; he did not even see the people who came out, staring and pointing, nor hear their whispers like the surf rising all about him. When he came to the gates of the barracks, however, he was made conscious of it, for the noise had increased: women were gabbling, and men pressed close, and there were cries of, "What is it? The king—he is wounded—he is dying!"

He turned to them, controlling himself, and said, "Good people, I am unharmed. Return to your homes."

A guardsman came running out to him, and Solomon said, "Bring to me Joel the son of Abner." Then, with impatience, he shouted to the crowd, which had not moved, "Do you not hear? Away with you! I am untouched; this is the blood of another."

"Lord, tell us what has happened!" cried a score of voices.

At that instant, Joel came out of the barracks, slinging on his sword belt. He stopped short, his mouth dropping open with horror at the sight of the king.

Solomon said, between his teeth, "Find Adonijah. Find my brother. Bring him here to me."

Joel said, "My lord, will you not come into the house? Shall I not call your physician?"

"No. I will remain here," said the king. "Do as I have commanded you."

There was a bench just inside the gate, and Solomon sat down heavily upon it. He stared at the dark sea of faces, feeling his breath rush in and out of his lungs, and the hammering of pulses in his temples. He could say no more. As for the people, at his words to Joel they had fallen silent, save for a whispering that went on and on among them, one telling another what was now clear: that the king's brother must have made an attempt on his life.

Within moments, a Pelethite pushed through the crowd and saluted the king. "My lord," he said, "the son of Haggith is within the Temple."

Solomon got to his feet. Now that he had rested, he felt the stiffness of his ride and of the fight; the muscles of his legs and back cracked with pain. Nevertheless, he motioned to Joel, saying, "Follow me, and bring with you a company that my brother may not escape. For as God lives, today he shall be put to death."

Once he had spoken those words aloud, a heavy depression settled upon his spirit, blanketing his anger. He set out for Moriah in the gathering twilight. Torches began to flame and the resinous fumes filled the air; the oily light wavered on still faces, and there was no sound save the shuffle of feet as the folk made way for him.

He came to the causeway and ascended it. He passed through the gates of the forecourt and climbed the steps, and entered between the two bronze columns, Boaz and Jachin. Behind him, guardsmen held up torches, and at his side went the son of Abner bearing a naked sword.

Before the Holy of Holies stood the bronze altar of burnt offerings, upon a dais reached by twelve stone steps. It was square, and at each of its upper corners a horn sprang out as had been commanded by the Lord Yahweh. Adonijah stood upon the topmost step with his back to the altar and one outflung hand resting on one of the horns. His face was gray, and his eyes bloodshot; he had been drinking heavily when the news had been brought him of Nebat's failure, by the man who had escaped. He looked down at the face of his brother, and his heart was cold within him; he felt neither fear nor remorse, but only the dead rage of enmity. Let him kill me, he thought, but he must do so upon the altar so that all Israel will turn from him in horror. Let him then feel what it is to be an outcast, to have all rent from his hands.

Solomon stopped, with his foot upon the lowest step. "Behold, brother," he said, touching the breast of his tunic. "Here is the blood of your servant, Nebat."

"I see only that it is not yours," Adonijah growled.

Joel said, "Let us drag him forth that his death may not profane the altar."

Solomon held him back with an outstretched arm. But Adonijah said, "Come—strike me down, for I prefer to die here before the Lord. All else you have taken from me that was mine, now take my life as well. Do not fear, my brother. I will not raise my hand, I will die as quietly as did Amnon before Absalom, on the day of the sheepshearing."

At these words, Solomon stood halted, like one in a nightmare, unable to move, and before his eyes rose the image of his brother Amnon at the feast table; this image faded and it was Adonijah who sat there, the sword blade standing within the bones of his skull, gaping wounds in his breast, and blood spattering the cloth and the plates and the arms of Solomon. Brother against brother! he thought. Am I come to this, that I should bear the mark of Cain?

Adonijah saw well that this passed within his mind, and laughed aloud, the familiar roaring laugh that echoed in the Temple's empty spaces. "You were ever a weakling," he jeered. "So said Joab, and so also said the Sheban whore. Go, then. Tell her that her plan has failed. She must get another to plot with her in my place."

Solomon heard him, but the words made no sense. He was numb; his legs would no longer bear him up and he took hold of Joel's arm to steady himself. He was like a man struck deep with an arrow, who, after the first stab of pain, feels nothing save the draining away of his strength.

He stared up at Adonijah with such eyes that the other fell silent. Then Solomon said, "I have been patient before now. When you proclaimed yourself king, I was forbearing. When you plotted with my mother, I still withheld my hand. You are worthy of death, but others have paid in your place for this day's work. For the sake of our father, David, I will not slay you. But you must go forth from the land, into Egypt or Moab or where you will. Never let me see your face again."

Adonijah looked at him, unbelieving and uncertain.

"Say no more," said Solomon, in a grating voice. "Go hence; you are free."

Adonijah drew a breath, his gaze sliding sidelong from Solomon to Joel and to the soldiers beyond. Biting his lips, he let go the horn of the altar at last, and slowly walked down the steps. Solomon neither moved nor spoke as his brother passed him, but with bent head listened to the footsteps recede until they were lost in the vast distance behind him.

When Balkis came to her house it was night. Two of the guardsmen had taken Zabud to the city of Jericho, walking their horses and supporting him in the saddle; the other two had escorted the queen. She dismissed them at her gate and stood for a moment in the garden, even as her servants came running out to her. There was a strange air over the city, of tension and expectation. Late as it was, lights burned everywhere, and in the streets knots of men gathered, talking in low voices.

The chief of her women, Shekiah, fat, mustached and muscled like a man, reached her first and cried out, "Ah! My radiant one— you are fouled and dirty. What have they done to you? Oh, the rumors that have reached us—how the Israelite king was set upon by murderers—how he has fought with his own brother—a barbaric and heathenish land!"

"Be silent, Shekiah," Balkis said, holding her brow. "Let us go within. Prepare a bath."

Shekiah clapped her hands and commenced driving the others back to the house. Then, she held out her arm for Balkis, motioning with the other at Arunazel the captain of the Sheban bodyguard, who burst into the garden at that instant with a dozen of his soldiers.

"Go," she shouted, "you are too late. She is returned. Always too late! Now send some of your dogs to see if they can unearth the accursed dwarf, Haran. But they will be too late for that, also."

"Haran?" said Balkis. "Why? What has happened to him?"

"Alas, my dove," Shekiah said, "what with all else that has happened—one thing piled upon another—that this, too, should have come about is not to be borne. The dead dog of an Ophirite has run away, no man knows whither, and worst of all he has stolen many of the queen's jewels. Nothing but affliction has come upon us since we arrived in this beastly land—"

"Peace!" said Balkis. With hurried steps she entered the house and went at once to her own bedchamber. Shekiah waddled close behind her. On an olivewood table beside the bed stood the small, ironbound chest which had contained some of her adornments: necklaces, earrings, bracelets and rings. The box was still open, the remains of its shattered lock hanging from the lid. Balkis looked within. There remained some baubles of little worth, but most of the jewels were gone, and with them the golden pendant, the amulet of Shams which was to have been her signal to Hadad the Edomite.

"Behold," puffed Shekiah, "it is even as I said. But Arunazel will capture the son of a dog—"

"No," said Balkis, almost inaudibly. And again, more firmly, "No. Do not search for him."

She leaned her weight on the rim of the box, while a wave of dizziness washed over her. As the drawing of a curtain lets in sunlight and transforms a room, the theft of the amulet illuminated the secret chamber of her heart and she saw now that her plotting had been in vain. If, still blind, she had used that golden signal as she had planned, she would have paid forever with remorse. And seeing herself plain, she felt a new emotion, a most unqueenly one—the pang of contrition. With her own careful snares, she had come near to destroying what was dearest to her in the world. Like a fool, she had mistaken her own desire and shot away all her arrows wide of the mark.

Shekiah still stood beside her, gaping in astonishment. Balkis said, sternly, "Did you not hear? Tell Arunazel the dwarf must not be harmed. Let him go. The hand of Shams is in this matter."

And as her woman departed, the queen covered her eyes with her hands, breathing within herself an inarticulate prayer of thanks to the Great Mother.

From the doorway, her steward said, in a frightened voice, "Lady —the king of Israel."

She looked round. Solomon stood before her. He had cleansed himself of his bloody garments, and wore a dark crimson kirtle and tunic and a belt of gold. On his face was a curious look, like a man listening for a sound in an empty house.

But this was nothing to her, for at the sight of him it seemed her heart would burst. She cried, "Solomon!" and ran to catch him in her arms; she began to weep, pressing her cheek against his neck, saying over and over like one distraught, "Beloved! Ah, my beloved!"

He took her by the arms, hesitating at first, and then held her a little away from him. "I have dealt with my brother," he said stiffly. "I have driven him forth."

She raised her head, clasping her hands about his neck and looking through her tears into his face. "Now deal with me, my lord," she sobbed.

He gazed at her, still with that strange expression as if he barely heard her. So great was her self-reproach and her need to speak, however, that she did not heed but went on, "Will you have the truth? Then listen, I came to Israel to overthrow you. I intrigued with your brother to help him rise up against you. I would have welcomed your death—until I saw you threatened. Why do you think I killed a man? And still I did not know. I did not know until now, seeing you safe before me, that you are my life and the breath of my nostrils, and my heart's blood. Do you hear? Do you understand? Now you may strike me down, if you will, for a traitress, but I love you."

His fingers tightened on her arms. His eyes had cleared, the shadow had lifted from them. "Balkis," he said. "Is this true?"

"That I plotted your downfall?"

"No, not that, for I care nothing for it. That you love me indeed?"

"It is so. You are my love, my brother, my husband . . ."

He crushed her to him, and so they stood swaying, lip to lip, thigh to thigh, avid for each other, blind with joy.

Then he said, "My sister, my love, the world stands between us."

"We will find a way," she whispered. "Never fear, but kiss me, that I may know you live, and are mine."

Once again, he bent to her, and in each other's lips they drank forgetfulness.

# part three

Rough red crags towered from the heated sands—the bones of Edom, wild and fierce as its people. At the foot of a mountain like a rosy cloud, near a water course marked by low, straggling oleanders and junipers, lay the camp of Hadad the son of Hadar. Black tents of goats' hair filled all the plain, and among them were staked camels and horses; the smoke of cooking fires darkened the sky, and a babel of voices, braying of asses, and barking of dogs ascended with the dust and smoke to the heavens.

The tents of Hadad's officers stood apart in a circle of their own, and in their center a large pavilion dominated the rest, not black like the others, but of blue-dyed Egyptian linen. Before it was planted the standard of the king of Edom. Within, it was all hung with fine silk and linen, and furnished with a bed of ebony, bronze lamps on stands of gold, and many cushions.

Here there was ample room for the council of war to meet. The chieftains of six tribes sat in a semicircle, eyeing each other blandly; they had taken oaths upon the altar of Sin and had witnessed the anointing of Hadad as king over Edom, yet they trusted each other no more than the lengths of their crooked swords. There were also two chieftains of Moab, who had come with swift horses and many foot soldiers, hoping for booty and ready to follow Hadad although they did not acknowledge his sovereignty. Hadad sat cross-legged at the head of this council; on his right hand were Kenaz, the son of his first wife, slender and gray-eyed, and an Egyptain captain, his blood brother Aman-Appa, who had come with a band of cavalry to help him recover his kingdom. On his left hand sat Adonijah the son of Haggith, and Joab the son of Zeruiah, with their armor-bearers behind them.

The years had worn Hadad as much sharpening wears away a good blade but increases its edge. Gone was his foppish Egyptian look and his courtly dress; he wore the many-colored cloak of the desert, and the ends of his braided hair fell among the thick strands of his beard. His brown face, weathered by camp and desert, eroded by disappointment and difficulties, had the fixed, wild look of a hawk in the madness of molt. Things had not gone easily or well with him. He had had to fight desperately for recognition and hew through a tangle of many loyalties, and even now five of the tribes refused to side with him, telling him courteously that if he won they would be glad to hail him as their ruler, but if not they would be no worse off paying tribute to Israel, a tribute which in any case they regained by plundering caravans between Ezion-geber and Jerusalem. The six who accepted him were strong—among them they sent more than fourteen thousand warriors into the field—but Hadad knew it would take little to set them at odds with each other and with him. Thus, he was forced to deal with them between conciliation and firmness, keeping his balance with difficulty.

He said, "The moment is at hand for which we have waited. Behold the amulet of the queen of Sheba."

He held out the golden disk. The dwarf, Haran, had brought it to the house of Joab, in Bethlehem, but Solomon had decreed exile for the son of Zeruiah also, so that he had departed at once for Edom. Adonijah, following almost upon his heels, had arrived this very day.

Hadad went on, "There remains only to determine the order of our attack, and where first to strike."

The Egyptian, Aman-Appa, said, "My lord and friend, I know not what others may say, but it is my right to go in the forefront with my horsemen wherever you make the first onset. I have taken an oath upon the altar of the blessed Osiris that I must be first in any battle."

"We will concede this honor to the king's friend," said Chief Timna drily. He was an elderly man whose face was almost black and whose sparse beard was like gray iron. He shook the silver bangles on his wrist, and continued, "If I may speak, then my counsel is that we attack the city of Beersheba, and burn it and plunder it. For it is a rich city, and has it not stood like a spearhead menacing Edom? Having laid it waste, we may then go on without fear of our backs standing unguarded."

Several of the other chiefs nodded approvingly, but Kenaz the son of Hadad, leaning forward with his hand on his dagger hilt, said hotly, "My father, this is the counsel of cowards!"

Hadad turned to his son with an expression which he strove to make stern, although his pride shone through it. "Be silent, my son," he said. "It is the place of the youngest to speak last."

"Ha, the young eagle," said Chief Timna, stroking his beard to conceal a smile. "Let him scream."

Kenaz said, "What! shall we go into Israel like thieves from the desert? When the smoke of Beersheba goes up, will not the king of Israel say, 'My men, join with me to put down these robbers and plunderers!' No, I say let us go up to the walls of Jerusalem and call upon him to come and fight with us, army against army—"

He broke off, flushing, for the chiefs were grinning and muttering to one another, and several laughed outright.

Then Joab, who had been watching Hadad from beneath his lowered eyelids, said smoothly, "My lord king of Edom, I pray you let me speak. Although I am a stranger, yet my name in war is not strange to some of you. And there is merit in what the young man says."

Hadad had scowled when Joab began, but at these last words his face softened, and he said, "Well, speak."

"It is true that plunder at the outset makes men less likely to fight," said Joab. "Those who have little stomach for war lose that little, and say, 'Let us go home with what we have, and offer thanks that we are yet alive.' Also it is true that when the first blow has been struck, many who might otherwise have deserted Solomon may follow him against an invader. The first assault must be directed against him, that all who waver may be smitten with fear. My advice, therefore, is that we march up into Israel with all our strength and invite Solomon out to parley with us. We will send word to the queen, Balkis, to persuade him to do this, and he will come, suspecting nothing and deluded by her, for he is a gentle and trustful man. When he has come to us, we will fall upon him and slay him."

When he had done, there was a silence, which was broken by Chief Iram, fat and bloated, whose little, glittering eyes were fixed upon Joab with aversion. "I hear the son of Zeruiah," he said. "His is a familiar voice. Was it not heard many years ago in Edom, above the wailing of women and the shrieks of the dying? What does he here at our council? He proposes that we betray the king of Israel, but how do we know he will not betray us? Who speaks with a double tongue, speaks doubly to all men."

Hadad said, "It is with my permission that he is here. He brought us the amulet from the queen of Sheba. It is his desire that Solomon be overthrown, and this works all ways to my intent. Also, he is here in the train of Adonijah, the prince of Israel, who is Solomon's enemy and therefore my friend."

"Then let the prince speak," said Chief Timna. "For I cannot take the barking of the dog to be the voice of his master."

Adonijah, gnawing the hairs of his mustache, looked balefully about him. "In my own land I would know how to answer such insolence," he said. "Let the son of Hadar tell his followers that they may be thankful I am here as an ally rather than an enemy."

"An ally?" piped Chief Magdiel, a wizened little man with a great, long beard. "First let our lord the king tell us what the Israelites bring us. Where are their soldiers?"

"Peace," said Hadad, with a frown. "The son of Haggith brought with him two hundred soldiers. Nevertheless, if he had brought two thousand, it would still not stand beside his worth. For when we go up against Israel, many will follow him and acclaim him their king, and thus will our task be made easier. And when we have conquered them, we will set Adonijah upon the throne that our own rule over Edom be better established. All this I have sealed with him, and with our ally Queen Balkis of Sheba."

He paused, and added quietly, "This should content you. And I will beg the son of Haggith to overlook the seeming discourtesy of the chieftains. For in Edom, our chiefs of tribes sometimes forget that they speak before the face of an anointed king, being plain and simple men. But let Adonijah say how this plan of Joab's seems to him."

"I say I like it not," Adonijah replied, glaring at Joab, in whom he saw at this moment the source of his humiliation and discomfiture. That Joab should have spoken first, and with so much assurance, galled him. He felt himself put upon with slights, from the moment Solomon had dismissed him into exile—in itself a kind of slight to his bitter pride, since he had been prepared for death—to this coming like a beggar to the camp of Hadad. Joab, he felt, had never treated him with respect. Old insults rankled in him like rusty arrowheads, and he said fiercely, "The plan is like him, venomous and two-faced. I have had enough of guileful ways. I am a plain man myself: let me but meet my enemy shield to shield, and I will hurl him into the dust. I say, let us march at once upon Beersheba, or upon any city in our path. Let us call on those within to join us and follow my standard. If they will not, let us put them to the sword and burn the city. This will draw out Solomon far better than any appeals to a parley. And when he comes, let us two fight it out and see which is the better man; as for his army, if he have one, it will not stand against our might."

Some of the chieftains nodded, and the Egyptian captain, Aman-Appa, said, "Well does the prince of Israel speak. I would count it an honor to go into battle with him."

Joab's lip twisted. He lifted his shoulders and said, "My lords, forgive me for speaking out. These words do my lord prince justice, for he has a noble heart. Yet he speaks without thinking. Why should we suppose that a burning city will bring out King Solomon? If he thinks it no more than a raid he will send Benaiah, the captain of his host, to deal with the matter. Nor is Solomon such a notable warrior that he will seek to settle the quarrel by hand-to-hand fighting with his brother upon the field. No, no, my lords, the son of Haggith has ever been overhasty, hotheaded, quick to leap—that is, where his honor calls. It is for a practiced soldier to look where his advantage lies, to husband his men, not to throw them uselessly into battle, to take his enemy unawares, and to use deceit and snares wherever he may. Or let Chief Magdiel tell me that I am wrong, for was it not he, thirty years ago, led me into an ambush and slew near half my men before I could escape?"

Chief Magdiel's withered face creased into a many-folded grin. "By my beard," he creaked, "I had forgot it. The son of Zeruiah speaks true. Old enemies know each other best."

"And you, Chief Timna," Joab went on, turning to the black patriarch, "did you not, at the battle of the River, by pretending flight, draw out the forefront of David's army and then fall upon them? You see, my memory is more than a bowshot long."

Chief Timna chuckled. "Even so. We sought not for honor in the old days, but for the winning of wars with little loss."

Hadad looked grimly at his council. Small pleasure did he take in hearing Joab speak thus, for his hold upon his followers was slight enough. Yet he must control himself, nor raise any issues that might cause dissension; it was his place to draw in all threads and bring them to concord. He said, "Well, this is all beside the point, delightful though it may be to recall the happiness of old battles. Of the two plans which have been proposed, it seems to me wiser to attack Beersheba first. If we have among us those who are faint of heart, the taking of plunder will encourage them. And when we speak of little loss, surely if the people of the city come out to follow Adonijah, we shall have fewer dead to count and mourn over."

Joab rested his chin upon his fist. Without troubling to conceal his contempt, he said, "My lord King Hadad, ever since I was a beardless boy I have known war. I was captain of a thousand when some who are here were not yet born. I was commander over King David's host for thirty years. I will say only one word here: if you will not defeat Solomon by subtlety, then it were wiser to wait. Much rests on the queen of Sheba. If by her devices she can bring Solomon to declare openly that he will wed her, then the kingdom of Israel will fall into our hands like a ripe fig ready for the eating. Swift impetuousness wins battles, my lord, but the two virtues of the man who wins wars are patience and cunning. As for those who think my plans treacherous, and thus dishonorable, be it remembered that there is no such word as treachery in warfare: all things are honorable when a throne is at stake."

Hadad's dark face grew darker still. "I thank the son of Zeruiah," he said, "for lessoning me in the usages of honor. Now I have heard all arguments upon either side, and I will take thought of them. By morning, I will give my decision. Against that time let all withdraw —all save the son of Haggith, for there are matters of polity which I must debate with him."

On that, the chieftains rose and each departed so that Hadad and Adonijah were left alone. Then Hadad, indicating that Adonijah should pour out wine, said, "You and I, prince, walk hand in hand in our way of thought. What lesser men cannot perceive is that a prince must live by openness in his dealings. For trust among rulers is the cement of kingdoms; let there enter suspicion and the fabric crumbles. Is this not so?"

Adonijah, glancing warily at the Edomite over the rim of his cup, nodded. "I would regret that any such should come between us," he said. "If it is your thought that I should offer sureties for our alliance when I am king—"

"Not sureties. No. I need no surety, for the son of Haggith has shown by his words at the council that he is straightforward, and a man of honor. But since we are speaking plainly, let me say that a prince must beware of his advisers. It is for him to determine whether their words to the world at large furnish his sureties—or not."

"Joab?"

"Just so. Bethink you, son of Haggith, how it appeared to us this day! Israel speaking with two voices, the captain never hesitating to put himself forward, nor to say, 'Adonijah speaks hastily . . .' How will it be when Adonijah is king? May not this man, who so lightly counsels the betrayal of King Solomon at a parley, also counsel Adonijah to forswear his word to Edom?"

He sat back, stroking his beard. Adonijah replied, in a grim tone, "That will not be."

"No?"

"No, son of Hadar, for as you have said we go hand in hand in all things. I will have speech with Joab. I have been patient too long."

He stood up and stretched, the large muscles of his forearms swelling with the movement. "I will find ways of binding him to my will," he said, and lifting the flap of the tent went out into the night.

The camp of the handful of Israelites who had followed Joab and Adonijah into exile stood a little apart from the tents of Edom, and by contrast was more orderly and quiet. For one thing, there were no women there, for the Law forbade them to come within a camp of warriors. Small fires burned, and many of the men were already asleep, while some sat about a lutist who played and sang a mournful desert melody.

Adonijah's tent was fully as large as that of Hadad, but bare and simple. Its only furnishings were some blankets and wool-stuffed pillows, and near the center a bronze lampstand of four wicks. The prince sat down beneath the lamp, and waited while Jehiel, his armor-bearer, went to fetch the son of Zeruiah. Mingled with the dull and smoldering anger in him was a kind of schoolboyish nervousness, and to squelch it he downed a cup of wine. He was pouring himself a second, when Joab, stooping, entered.

"Your servant is here, my lord," he said, but there was scant humility in his tone. "I was about to lie down to sleep, but for the old, sleep is often long in coming."

"Let the son of Zeruiah listen," said Adonijah, with a lowering glance. "I have heard his biting words before and have not raised my hand. But in council with another king, Joab would do better to keep silence, or to say what he has to say after I have spoken."

Joab looked long at the prince. Then, with deliberation, he sat down opposite him. "I am old, son of Haggith," he said. "And I am weary, as well. I have nothing to show for the years in which I served your father save a few pieces of armor. Do not interrupt, for you are not yet privy to the voice of God and there is no other but myself to tell you the truth. You are as a child. There is in you no power for ruling, nothing save greed and childish arrogance. Yet you are your father's son, and I have sworn to uphold his blood and line. But do not think to come among the councils of men with your folly.

See where the consequences of your own acts have brought you—into exile, and myself along with you. If you had taken my advice, if you had waited, we should not be begging charity of this Edomite upstart; no, you would have your woman to bed, and the crown as well. Now leave these matters to me, let me guide you and be your voice, and we will yet triumph. But if you do not . . ." He opened his eyes wide, so that it was as if lamps, hidden all this while, were suddenly unveiled. There shone forth from his face a clear light of malevolence, pure evil, without conscience or rein. He no longer cared what he said, nor was he concerned to mask his true self, and for that single instant Adonijah sat stunned and powerless before the strength of his spite. "If not," continued Joab, in a flat voice, "then I shall depart. I will return into Israel, though they slay me for it, and I will go before Solomon and warn him of your coming. I do not threaten idly, as you should know. And now I swear it—I will bring you all down with me into Sheol."

He struck his palm flat against the earthen floor.

It needed only that sound, like a slap in the face, to awaken Adonijah. Wrath boiled up within the prince, blinded him and choked him. He gripped the hilt of his dagger.

"Double-dealer and serpent," he said thickly. "Ever have you tried to push me, to bend me to your purposes. To Sheol? Go you before, then!"

He seized Joab by the hair and dragged his head down to the ground. He plucked out his dagger like a madman and stabbed, point downward, with all his might. The blade ripped through Joab's throat and pinned him to the earth. One bubbling, horrible cry burst forth. The dagger tore free. The son of Zeruiah rolled on his back, his mouth wide, another gaping mouth below, from which the blood spurted, black in the lamplight. He drew up his knees in a single convulsion, still trying to cry out but drowning in his own blood.

Adonijah drew back, and stiffly got to his feet. He stared at the body of Joab, panting, and slowly wiped his dagger upon his kirtle. Then he went to the tent flap. Outside, a group of men had gathered silently, drawn by the last cry of the son of Zeruiah, but afraid to come nearer. One of them was Adonijah's armor-bearer.

"Some of you, come within," said the prince, in a voice still clogged with passion. "Take out this carrion and bury it. And you, Jehiel, go to the tent of the lord of Edom, Hadad the son of Hadar, and say to him from me, 'The son of Haggith bids me tell you that surety has been found. There is no more dissension within the camp of Israel.'"

For Solomon and Balkis the days and nights passed swiftly, golden
and timeless, hour merging into hour. All that had been before this
enchantment of love was forgotten, all that might yet come was end-
lessly postponed. There remained only the pleasure of their new-
found happiness, an exploration infinite and delectable.

Solomon's only thought was to please his love. He delighted to
bring her gifts, to make her laugh and see her dark eyes glow. He
joyed to look upon her in all her moods, now stormy, now languid,
to behold her rich body amorous or satiated. He would take her face
between his hands and study it; the line of her lip like the fine curve
of a Syrian bow, the depths of her eyes, the arched wings of her
nostrils; and when she said, "Why do you stare at me thus?" he
would reply, "I wish to fix you in my mind, so that when I am apart
from you I may recall you entire."

She had a small brown mole on one cheek. "Even my blemishes?"
she said, laughing.

"Even those, for they make you a woman. You must not be too
perfect." And he kissed the mole, and went from kiss to kiss until
once more they sank rapturously into each other's embraces.

Or he would lie, watching her from beneath his lowered eyelids,
by daylight or lamplight, never tiring of the sight of her, hoarding
up images to dream upon, miserly with his treasures: Balkis passing
a golden comb through her thick hair, her arms lifted, her head a
little on one side, the heavy tresses falling below her shoulders;
Balkis throwing a light scarf about her rosy-tipped breasts, her na-
kedness shining beneath it like the sun veiled in mist; Balkis pouting

at her mirror, poised on one leg, the other bent, touching with one finger a bruise on her throat where he had bitten her, and eyeing him reproachfully.

Or, she would cuddle beside him like a full-fed cat, twisting to find a comfortable position, nibbling his ear, tickling him, giggling like a schoolgirl, whispering to him, "Tell me once again how beautiful I am." And he would say, piling one extravagance upon another, "The curves of your hips are like necklaces, the handicraft of an artist. Your navel is a round bowl, in which liquor is never lacking. Your belly is a heap of wheat fenced in with hyacinths. Your two breasts are like two fawns, twins of a gazelle. Your neck is like a tower of ivory; your eyes are pools in Heshbon—"

She would interrupt him mischievously, "Heshbon? Where is Heshbon? And how may I be certain it is not some pesthole where the pools are muddied and brown with water weed? No, no, I will have none of that!"

Then he must stop her mouth with his, and force her to silence, but not to sobriety.

Even with others, they were yet alone, confined within a kind of magic circle that had power to keep out all intrusions. At dinner, their hands would touch over some dish; in crowded halls, smiling and conversing with their companions, their eyes would meet and exchange promises. It was as if all else in the world, all other people and other places, were nothing but a gay tapestry against which they moved: many-colored but lifeless, the only life being that which sprang between these two. To pass before this tapestry was no more than an interlude, dividing the hours of reality when they could be together, in his high, airy, private room, in her bedchamber, or on spicy and delicious nights in her garden.

It was here Sittar came upon them, early one evening, sitting side by side on the stone rim of the cistern and dropping pebbles into the water. Balkis sat close to her lover, his arm about her waist, their cheeks touching, chuckling together to see the stars shiver in the ripples. When Sittar spoke, they looked at him with casual eyes as if he were no more than a stone, or a tree, in the twilight.

"Awake!" he said, somewhat testily. "Behold me. Balkis! It is your brother, Sittar, who speaks to you."

"How might I mistake that croaking voice and ugly face?" said Balkis lazily.

Sittar sighed. He came to the opposite side of the tank and said, more gently, "May I sit? I am overcome by all this royalty."

"Sit or stand, as it pleases you," Balkis said.

"No, Sittar, heed her not," said Solomon. "Come, sit near us. For-give me that I have seen so little of you."

"I have had other distractions," said his friend, grinning. Then, sobering, he went on, "Listen to me, lovers. I have not come to break in idly upon your dalliance. I have come because I love you both well, and this may not continue."

They said nothing, but smiled at him as doting parents upon a child who says its first words. He said, in irritation, "Ilmuqa support me. Do you know what is said throughout the city? That Solomon is mad, or bewitched by my sister. Do you know that none dared come and tell you this, save myself? Have you seen the faces of your counselors, Solomon, or heard their mumblings? Have you noticed Benaiah, who watches you as a whipped dog its master, tail between legs? No! By the arrow of Ilmuqa, you have seen nothing—"

"We have seen each other," said Solomon with a smile. Then he put out his hand. "Alas, I meant not to wound Sittar. I know he thought only of us. We have talked of the matter, in truth we have."

"But you have come to no decision."

"Not yet."

Sittar rose, placing his hand affectionately on Solomon's shoulder. "Be guided by me," he said. "Matters cannot go on thus, for over all this land there is a shadow. I have heard men speak against my friend, the king, and against my sister, calling her a seducer and a harlot. None of this can end well. Ask counsel of your god, Solomon."

Solomon heaved a sigh, and with one hand swept the last of the pebbles into the water. "I have done so," he said. "The day following Adonijah's attempt on my life, I called Zadok the high priest, and bade him bring to me the oracle pouch and to consult the Stones of the oracle. But the Lord did not answer me. That night I passed before the Holy of Holies, hoping for a dream from God, but my dreams were voiceless, full of vague shapes, empty of meaning. Then, at last, I sent one to find the prophet Nathan to demand that he inquire of the Lord for me, although it went much against my will to do so. But Nathan is dead."

"That old man who stopped us on the hillside?" asked Balkis.

"That was he. He died in the night, in his hut under the mountain of God. Now, therefore, since the Lord withholds his voice from me I do not know what I should do. And to speak the truth, I am content to do nothing." He clasped Balkis' hand. "Let us wait. It may be some thought will come to me, some way of satisfying my people that a marriage between us does not threaten them."

Sittar turned to Balkis. "And you, my sister?"

"I?"

"Are you not the priestess of the Threefold One? Have you inquired of her?"

At that, Balkis cast down her eyes. "Between her and the Father there is enmity in this land. I know not whether she would hear me."

Solomon drew her tightly to him, brushing her hair with his lips. Even the slightest tinge of sadness in her voice filled him with compassion and sympathy. He said, "Tell me of your goddess. Why do you call her the Threefold One?"

"She has three aspects in which she appears to us. She is Shams, the Life-giver, the radiant bride from whose loins comes the young Baal, the youthful god of the spring sowing. She is also Ashtar, the Morning Star, patroness of lovers, who by the holy act of love brings young goats and lambs leaping forth. And lastly, she is the Dark One, whose name I may not speak, the Great Sow, eater of her own young . . ."

She shivered, and made a sign with her fingers, moving away from Solomon as she did so. He reached for her, but she put her hands against his chest and went on, "Listen. I did not wish to speak of this before, knowing your mind and the jealousy of your god. But now you have told me your god is silent. Ashtar is kind to lovers, she who is herself the Beloved. If you would go with me—"

"Anywhere!"

"Up into a high place where we might sacrifice to her. For we must do it together. And afterward, lie down together and await whatever dream she sends us. Would you do that?"

For a time, Solomon sat motionless. He knew well that this moment had been inevitable; indeed, when Zadok, casting the sacred lots, had shaken his head finding no answer, although Solomon rephrased his question many different ways, then in the king's mind had first risen the thought that if Yahweh turned away his face, he might search elsewhere for aid. Had not Saul, in the same predicament, gone to the woman of Endor? He had put the thought out of his head, for the Law was clear: to avoid diviners and those who practiced sorcery. Yet he had felt not so much horror at himself for the thought, as surprise at his lack of horror; to what lengths would a man not go, driven by a desire sharper than any spear?

And was the Law not equally clear on this point? "If any entice you, saying, 'Let us serve alien gods,' you must not yield to him, nor heed him; nay, your own hand must be the first against him to put him to death."

The Law might seem hard and cruel but to those who loved

Yahweh and worshipped him, it was just and right. Nevertheless, all these considerations paled and faded and were without significance before the love Solomon bore Balkis. He could more easily cut off his right hand than deny her, and he knew now for sober truth what he had once sung as no more than a poet's fancy, that love was indeed stronger than death, stronger than the Pit, mightier even than the Law.

He clasped Balkis' hands, and said, "I will do as you desire. Wherefore not? Is not my heart yours? Are we not one flesh? Say what you would have me do."

"Then let it be this night," Sittar put in. "For the sooner it is attempted, the better for us all."

Now that he had given his assent, Solomon felt a twinge of doubt, a slight inward quaking which, however, he repressed. Had he not once said, "All gods may be only the several faces of the One God?" Why should that not be true? He said, "What is needful for the sacrifice? It might be wiser to wait, lest we attract too much attention, for there may be some who will protest and make an outcry at my doing this."

"Little is needed," said Balkis. "A handful of incense, some wine, and a young he-goat. Nor need any come with us save some of my women. Sittar is right; let us go at once."

She sprang up lightly, stooping to kiss his mouth. "I will have all things prepared. Wait you here. As for you, my brother, leave us. By dawn, it may be, we will have some word to satisfy you."

"Oh, I am easily satisfied," Sittar said, with a shrug.

With that, he left them there, and walked by winding streets to the hill where stood the palace of the king. He ascended the outer stair to the rooftop, and there he found Abishag waiting for him.

She had been sitting quietly in the gloaming, accustomed as she was to patience, softly playing simple figures upon her lyre, and contenting herself with the new peace that had come to her in these last weeks. For ever since that evening when Sittar had confessed his love to her, her heart had found rest; she told herself that she loved Solomon no less, but the aching loneliness was now assuaged by friendship and sympathy. It was, she felt sure, no more than that. Sittar was a good companion, high-spirited and merry, ready to listen, or if she wished to be silent, as ready to talk and full of tales of the places he had visited and the strange sights he had seen. And if, now and then, he took her hand or sat more closely to her in the cool evening wind, where was the harm in that, between friends?

At the sound of his step, her heart leaped. She put aside the lyre and said, "I have been asking myself if Sittar would come this evening. For it is later than usual."

"I have been doing good works in the world," he replied lightly. He threw himself down on the divan beside her, and added, "Is it possible Abishag would miss me if I did not come?"

"Do not be cruel. I would be very lonely without Sittar."

"Cruel?" He smiled ruefully. "Then I must be cruel some day. For I cannot stay in Israel forever. Have you not thought that my sister must return to Sheba, to the duties of her throne, and I with her?"

She was silent for a space, and then she said in a low, faltering voice, "I had forgotten. I have been content to take each day as it came, and find joy with my friend."

He bent toward her. "Am I no more than Abishag's friend?" he whispered. "Friends may part, knowing they will meet again, content with messages and the memory of past pleasures. But if I go I will leave half of myself behind. Would you have me tear myself in two?"

She shook her head vehemently, as if to free herself, and rose up; she went to the parapet, pressing her temples with her finger tips. "No," she said. "Do not speak so."

He came behind her, and said into her ear, "I must. Call me what you will, I am not your friend. I swear to you on my life, I love you too dearly for friendship. Come with me, Abishag. Come to Sheba. Be my wife."

He put his arms about her and kissed her neck and shoulder, and she did not resist. Only she said, "No. I cannot."

"But why?" he cried. "What demon holds you from me?"

Still within his embrace, she said, "I am the daughter of my people. I cannot follow after strange gods."

"But you may keep your own god. I will make you an altar for him in my house."

"I cannot leave my own land."

He pressed her closer. "Stubborn and stiff-necked, like all your people. Why do I yet love you? I am a fool."

She leaned her head back against him, and said, "I do not even know if I love Sittar. I do not know what I feel. There is confusion in me."

"Listen to me, Abishag."

She lifted her head a trifle. "What is that?" she said, dreamily. "Look yonder, at the heights of Olivet."

A half-score of twinkling yellow dots shone above En-rogel, as of torches going up in the distance.

Sittar said, "That is my sister going up to sacrifice to her goddess, on the heights. Solomon is with her."

"Solomon?"

"He has no such scruples as you. I persuaded them to try if the goddess Ashtar might give them an answer to their problems, and show them how they might wed. And if they were to wed, would this not make things easier for Abishag? If our two countries were joined—"

Her body stiffened in his arms. She said, "You did that? You?"

He took her by the arms and tried to turn her about, but she pulled away from him. He said, "Abishag! What is it? Have I not acted for the best? Surely, if Solomon's god will give him no answer why should they not approach the gods of Sheba?"

But even as he spoke, a wound opened in his breast; he knew that all defense was useless, even though he did not understand her reasons.

She said to him, "You say that you love me. Do you call this love? To seduce the king of Israel from the God of his father? To turn his heart after false gods and divide him still further from his people? A fool? You are right—you are a fool, if you are not a traitor as well, seeking to destroy us."

"Abishag!" he cried.

"Come not after me," she said, fiercely. "Why did you enter this land? Since you came, you and your sister, there has been nothing but evil here. How can I trust you? What did you say—that you would build an altar for me in your house? Liar! How long would it be before I found myself put to abominations among your people?"

Her voice broke, and she sobbed painfully. He raised his arms, taking a halting step toward her, and she turned and fled, running blindly down the stair in the dark.

For a long time, Sittar stood numb, unable to pursue her or to move from that spot. Then he sank down on the parapet. He looked toward the heights of the Mount of Olives, where a fire now flickered like a star.

"Solomon, my brother," he said, glumly, to himself, "indeed I did wrong to send you to entreat of a goddess. For who can tell how to please a woman?"

On the rounded knoll at the top of the Mount of Olives stood an ancient altar of stone in the midst of a grove of silvery trees. Here, once, the Canaanites had worshipped the *baal* of the olives, and there still stood, behind the altar, the moldering wooden phallic pole

which they had used to deck with garlands of leaves. To this spot
came Solomon and Balkis, each with a hand upon one of the horns
of a young he-goat, and behind them ten women with torches, led
by the robust Shekiah who bore a skin of wine, two cups, a brazier
and tripod, and a bag of incense, all which she carried as if they
had no weight. It was by now full dark, with brilliant stars powder-
ing the velvet sky.

They entered the grove, and Shekiah at once set some of the
women to cutting wood and building a fire on the hearth of the
altar. Bronze bars, green with age, still remained embedded in the
top, although two of the horns of the altar had broken off. When
the fire was burning brightly, Shekiah set up the tripod and filled
the brazier with hot coals, and over them cast a double handful of
incense, so that a heavy plume of sweet smoke arose. Then, from
her girdle, she drew a long bronze knife which she handed to Solomon. She held the goat between her knees, and taking its head by
one horn and by the beard easily twisted it to expose its throat.

Solomon turned the knife between his fingers. His eyes met those
of the woman, in which a subtle smile lurked—small, glittering, black
eyes like onyxes embedded in the creased fat of her face.

"Strike, O king," she said.

Was there mockery in her tone? Nothing of it showed in her expression. He glanced at Balkis: there was, on her face, a rapt, attentive look, inward-turned, of deep concentration.

He laid his hand on the goat's forehead, and thrust the knife into
the great artery of the neck, making the sacrifice expertly. At once,
Balkis held out a cup and caught some of the blood as it spurted
forth. He expected her to dash it to the side of the altar, as the
Levites did for a burnt offering; instead, she waited while Shekiah,
letting the goat's body fall, took the wineskin and poured wine into
the other cup. Balkis mingled the contents of the two cups, and held
out one of them for Solomon.

The women had formed a circle round about the grove, facing
outward and holding their torches high. They began to chant, very
softly, nor could Solomon distinguish any of the words. Then
Shekiah, without flaying or cutting up the goat, placed it on the bars
above the fire, poured a little wine over it, and threw a handful of
incense upon it.

Balkis took Solomon's hand and led him to the altar. They stood
hand in hand, holding their cups, and Balkis said, "Serpent-bodied
Ashtar, thou Lady of the Doves, accept this offering."

She raised her cup, saying to Solomon, "Do likewise," and drank.

A shudder passed over him, for to drink the blood of a sacrifice was forbidden. But he had come so far, to stop now would be senseless. He put the cup to his lips. The wine had a sickly taste, sweet and salt, at which his gorge rose. Yet he drank as Balkis did, and threw down the cup.

The chanting grew louder, rose to a peak, and ended. All at once the women plunged their torches into the earth, extinguishing them. There remained only the leaping flames of the altar.

Balkis drew Solomon to the ground. She unclasped her girdle and lay down upon him, uttering little broken cries and incoherent words. The scent of her body mingled with the smell of blood, of charring flesh and burning hair, and the heavy sweetness of incense. Lust rose in him, struggling against his repulsion; he embraced her, shivering uncontrollably, knowing in her the dreadful nature of the Love Goddess, in whom are mixed sweetness and disgust, grotesqueness and grace, pain, joy, and despair.

Then, having known each other, they fell asleep, and in the deepest part of the night a dream came to Solomon. It was in the shape of a woman, very tall and white-faced, her hair in ringlets falling to her shoulders, her breasts bare, and about her hips a skirt of many flounces. In one hand she held a scourge, in the other a cup, and on either side of her, young goats gamboled and frisked.

He searched her face, certain that he knew her, thinking she might be Balkis in another guise. He said, "Have I not seen you in the hills and valleys of my people?"

"I was here before you or your people, or the god of your people," she replied, laughing soundlessly.

"What would you of me, then?" he asked.

"Rather say what you would have of me, for you have called me. You have sacrificed on my altar, drunk the blood of my covenant, burned incense before me. Behold, here I am."

He saw now that there was a serpent coiled round her waist, and the sight of it filled him with loathing. Yet he was drawn to her, for she was very beautiful. He said, "I would have and have not."

"Then," she replied, "you must forsake the ways of your father and follow after me."

"And if I will not?"

Before his eyes she changed; her face withered, and became that of an ancient hag, fanged, whiskered, red-eyed and malicious. "Do as you have a mind to do," she croaked. "In the end all things come to me."

He was overcome with dread. "I am the king," he said—or tried to say, but his voice choked in his throat. He began to flee from her, but ever she followed him, chuckling. He fled through the mazes of his dream, and emerged suddenly into waking, and daylight.

He sat up, wiping his wet face with a cold hand. Balkis lay asleep beside him, her naked limbs huddled together against the chill of morning. Her face was innocent, the long lashes dark on her cheeks, the lips a little pouted out, her hair tumbled about her face and a few strands caught like spider web across her mouth. As he watched her a pang of pity and love touched him deep, as of a sharp lute-quill picking at his heartstrings.

He looked about. The altar fire was dead; the women asleep beneath their cloaks. As for his dream—he dug the heel of his palm into his eyes. It was fading. There had been a woman in his dream, but what she had said he could not remember, nor what they had done, save that he had fled from her while still desiring her.

A clank of metal came to his ears, and voices, one calling, "My lord! My lord Solomon!"

Hastily, he covered Balkis with her robes. He stood up and set his own garments to rights, smoothed down his hair with both hands, and passed between two of the sleeping women to leave the grove. Up the hillside, half a dozen armed men were coming, led by Benaiah. The captain of the host was clad in a bronze corselet of overlapping scales, and a horned helmet of leather and iron. He went as quickly as he might, leaning on his spear and stopping from time to time to call.

Solomon went to meet him. "Why does my captain come armed for war?" he said. "And how knew you I was here?"

Benaiah looked at him, and past him at the still forms about the grove, and at the brazier and the black, shriveled husk of the sacrifice seen through the gray trunks of the olive trees.

He said, in a worried voice, "My lord, I came searching for you at the palace before sunrise. None knew where you might be until the Sheban prince, the son of Merisamis, came down and told me you were . . . busied upon the heights of Olivet. I did not wish to break in upon you, but, my lord, the news cannot wait—"

"What news?"

Benaiah swallowed, as if the words stuck in his throat. Then he said, "War. Red war is in the land."

Solomon's strength drained from him, and it was as if a cold hand closed upon him. He said, "Adonijah? Is it he?"

"I do not know, my lord. But a horseman rode in to me this very morning bringing word that a great army out of Edom had entered

Israel. Beersheba is burned, and the countryside about it laid waste, and now they march northward, more numerous than grasshoppers."

Solomon closed his eyes for a moment, to collect himself. "Go down a little way and wait for me," he said.

He returned to the grove, and found Shekiah with her back against a tree, her arms folded across her mighty breasts, her eyes open and fixed upon him shrewdly. "You heard?" he said.

The woman nodded silently.

"Very well. Awaken your mistress and return with her to the house. Tell the news, and say to her that nothing else would have taken me from her side."

He moved to go. Shekiah whispered, "My lord king."

"What is it?"

"What shall I tell her of your prayer? Was there a sign? For she will surely ask me . . ."

He frowned, and all at once the words of his dream flashed into his mind: "You must forsake the ways of your father and follow after me."

He covered his face with his hand. "Tell her nothing," he said. "Nothing."

He rejoined the son of Jehoiada, and went down the hillside with him into a city already buzzing with the word of war.

The host of Israel assembled about Jerusalem under the captains of hundreds and the captains of thousands. Not all the tribes were there, but the men of Judah and Benjamin, of Ephraim, Manasseh, and Gad appeared, as well as some hundreds of Reuben and Gilead. As for the rest, messengers would carry the word to them, and they would rest upon their arms waiting to hear if they should be needed for reinforcement. The men of Simeon, those who could do so, had already met the Edomites and their allies and had been scattered: they were, in any case, mostly nomadic villagers.

Solomon stood on a hillock outside the gates, in council with the leaders of the army. He wore a gilded coat of scale-mail, with bronze greaves and a bronze helmet, all gilded and set with plaques of turquoise, and over his mail a fringed cloak of Tyrian dye hemmed with gold. His mien was kingly, and he showed nothing of the dismay and gloom in which his spirit was sunk.

It was clear Yahweh frowned upon him. He, who had thought only of peace, had brought disaster to the land; he, whose hands were shaped to the lyre and the pen, must now be apt for war. Yet, in spite of his guilt and fear, he remained impenitent and rebellious.

He would not bow to this doom, he told himself, but would fight for the one bright thing left him—his love for Balkis. This alone mattered, this alone was worth the price of the world. And if in the end he must abide by the oracle of his dream, then he would do so in despite of all.

He clenched his teeth, looking down on the captains who stood shifting and muttering, more than a score of them. "So, then," he said, "you have come at my command and now you are uncertain whether to follow me?"

Eliam the son of Ahithophel, a grizzled old man with a deep chest and long, hairy arms, stood in the forefront. He had been one of David's Thirty, whose names were legendary in the land; he had also followed Adonijah when the prince proclaimed himself king, although because of his honorable history Solomon had refrained from punishing him. He said, "None of us have said we will not follow our lord the king. Only, some of us have said, 'Tell us whether these rumors are true which have come to our ears, that the king's heart has been turned away from the Lord our God, and that he has sacrificed to an alien god?' For as Ittai of Gibeah has said just now, how can Israel hope for victory if the Lord is not with us?"

He glanced, as he said this, at his companion, a man with black, heavy brows that met over a sickle-shaped nose. He was captain over a thousand from Benjamin.

Before the king could reply, a tall, proud-looking man clashed his sword against the rim of his shield. His name was Eleazar the son of Shammah, and he was a Judahite. "Does the king heed the clamor of dogs?" he cried. "Is there no image of the teraphim in the house of the son of Ahithophel? Why should we inquire how the king sacrifices? He has been anointed of God."

"I hear many arguments in the words of Eleazar," said Ittai the Gibeahite, in a deep bass voice. "Yet I do not hear him say that Israel must be led by an idolator. Was it not so, my lord king, that the king's own mother, Bathsheba, spat in his face not two days ago, and has since closed herself up in her chamber, and comes not forth, saying that her son runs after false gods? Or is this a lie spread by ill-wishers?"

"It is no lie," said Solomon. His words fell like stones into the pool of faces, and a circle of silence spread around him. "Those who would follow my mother into war may do so. As for the rest, I say to you that whatever I have done I am yet the Lord's anointed, the king over Israel. Our land is in danger, it has been invaded. Is this the time to quarrel? Rather let us stand firm like a band of brothers, to destroy the Edomite lest we all perish."

He was aware, as he finished, that he had not won them. Am I my father's son? he thought bitterly. *He* was called the Beloved of Israel, the Star of Bethlehem, the Lamb of Judah—by all those endearing names was he known. What was his art, that men forgave him all his sins? They would have gone with *him,* or if not, they would have said to him as they had said at Gob, "Go not into battle, for you shall not quench the lamp of Israel."

Or, he thought, am I rather my mother's son: my mother, whose husband David had sent to be slain, whose first-born was taken by God as a sin offering? And he felt again on his cheek his mother's spittle, and heard her voice strident with fury, crying, "Let me see your face no more! I have no son!" Israel rejected him, as his mother had rejected him, and as the God of the Law rejected him.

Elika the Gadite, a man whose deeply grooved face bore a perpetually sour smile, was speaking. "My lord king, our loyalty is not in question. Only tell us for whom we are to fight, the Lord Yahweh, or the queen of Sheba and her gods."

A giant of a man, whose long hair was braided on either side of a heavy-jawed face, shouted in a voice of thunder, "What insolent talk is this?" He was a Bethlehemite, Dodi the son of Elhanan, a man renowned in war. He went on, "The king is near of kin to us, the men of Judah. We will not question, nor will we cast dirt at him. Lead us into battle, son of David!"

A growl went up from many of his partisans, but there were equally menacing words and looks from others of the captains who opposed him. Elika the Gadite said, "Think not to overawe us by noise." Then Eleazar the son of Shammah bellowed, "Go to your homes, dogs of Benjamin and Gad! You were ever known as cowards, skulkers, hangers-back." Here and there swords were half out of their sheaths, and Benaiah, standing beside the king with a frown on his face, motioned covertly to Joel the son of Abner, as if to bid him be ready for a fray. Then Ittai the Gibeahite, cried out, "Let the king give up the Sheban woman and we will follow him!"

At this, the patience of the king burst its bonds. "Silence!" he roared. Such rage was in his face that those nearest him involuntarily gave back. He glared at them, and said, "Listen to me, you captains. Not at the bidding of any man will the king of Israel give up a crumb of bread from his hand. Do you think to force me to your will, and then have me lead you?" He drew a breath in between his teeth, and continued, "As for the queen of Sheba, she is not your concern; neither are my dealings with her to be pried into by you. Not the Lord God himself may put me aside from her. Do not seek, therefore, to make yourselves my guardians."

At these words, many quailed and moved yet further back as if fearing that the lightning would fall upon him and them. Then Eliam the son of Ahithophel seized the battle horn that hung at his belt, and blew a blast, and shouted, "We have no portion in Solomon! We have no share in the son of David. Each man to his tent, O Israel!"

He turned and strode away, and with him went Ittai of Gibeah, Elika the Gadite, and many others.

Then Solomon said, "May God do so to me and more if I go not out to battle this day. If I must, I will go alone. But if there are any who have no fear, let them stand with me."

Dodi the son of Elhanan, lifting his heavy spear that was like a weaver's beam, said, "If there be one man of Judah who hesitates, let him speak now and die."

And Joel the son of Abner said, "The king has no need to ask of his bodyguard, for we will follow him as we have sworn."

Solomon looked at them both with gratitude. Sittar came up to him, and took his hand, and said, "My brother, I will go with you and be your armor-bearer, since Zabud is not yet healed."

"Not so," said Solomon. "If, as I fear, Adonijah is with the Edomites, and if by the will of God he vanquishes me and comes to Jerusalem as king, then will your sister—and more than that, Abishag the Shunammite—be in danger. I pray you, my brother, remain behind with your Shebans and guard them for me. This is a hard task since my brother is hot for the fight, but will he do so?"

Sittar bit his lip, but at last he nodded.

Solomon dropped his voice almost to a whisper. "I will not see Balkis before I depart, for my heart is already heavy enough with sorrow and I fear lest the sight of her unman me. But say to her that I love her well, and that if my God—or hers—permit, I will return."

He embraced the prince, and then faced Benaiah. "Commander of my host," he said, "you have little to command. Will you yet come with me?"

Benaiah looked sternly but affectionately at him. "As the Lord lives," he said, "wherever the king shall be, whether for death or life, there will his servant be."

"Come, then," Solomon said firmly. "Let us delay no longer."

He went swiftly to his chariot, while the trumpets sounded.

Eliahba, the youngest son of Elhanan and brother of Dodi, took the king's shield and three javelins, and mounted beside him.

There followed Solomon that day six hundred Cherethites and Pelethites of his bodyguard, all with gilded helmets and shields of gold, four thousand men of Judah, and two thousand of Ephraim and Manasseh. But all the rest remained behind, encamped near the city and unable to decide amongst them whether to return to the city or to stay and await the outcome of the battle.

Sittar rode sadly back to the city under an ominous sky blood-red
with sunset. He had accompanied Solomon as far as Bethlehem
where, with a final embrace, his friend had set out with the soldiers
along the hill road toward Hebron. Sittar chafed under his promise,
for it pleased him little to remain idle while others were busy in a
bickering. At the same time, to remain under the same roof with
Abishag gave him a melancholy joy, even though she had neither
met with him nor spoken to him since that unfortunate evening on
the rooftop.

He urged his mount between the tents, listening glumly to the
clamor of argument that went on almost everywhere and thinking
to himself that there was much resemblance between these quarrel-
some, independent, and obstinate Israelites and his own people who,
although they gave the utmost in adoration to their queen and goddess, yet persisted in going their own ways under their clan chieftains whenever it suited them. It would not be so strange for a
Sheban to settle here, to live amongst these people and be one of
them. As for their God—Sittar shrugged to himself, for he was one
who never concerned himself unnecessarily with the gods, giving
them their due when it was needful and for the rest considering
that they had their own celestial affairs to look after and he had his
earthly ones. Perhaps, then, if he were to become one of them
Abishag might some day look with favor at him once again. But
there! who knew what was in a woman's heart? Mysterious indeed
were the ways and rites of the goddess. He sighed, and kicked
moodily at his horse's belly as they went up under the square gate-

way; then he patted its neck and murmured, "Forgive me, friend, the fault lies not with you."

He rode to the house where his sister dwelt, and gave his horse into the hands of a servant. He went in and there found Shekiah sitting in the hall with her hands on her thighs. When she saw him, she said, "My lord prince, I would that we were away from this land, or that you had never come raiding here in the first place, for my poor mistress has neither drunk nor eaten since morning but remains in her room alone and will see no one, and as for me, worry and care have shriveled me to a skeleton."

He looked sardonically at her, and replied, "Up, woman! There is still a little meat on your bones. I will go in and see the queen my sister, and when I come out do you have some food ready for me, for I also have eaten nothing."

"But the queen has commanded that none shall disturb her—"

"Shekiah," said the prince, sharply, "do not cross me this night, for my day has been long and dismal. Away with you. Let your disobedience to my sister be on my head, and do not seek to make yourself more than you are."

She eyed him, and saw that his temper was indeed stretched. She made a ponderous obeisance and went off. Sittar passed through the hall and ascended to the great bedchamber above.

The room was full of dusk. Sittar stood blinking on the threshold, and after a moment or two made out his sister lying face down on the floor.

"Balkis," he said, hesitantly.

Slowly she raised her head. "Is it Sittar?"

He went to her and fell on his knees beside her. She pushed herself up a little way, and he put his arms about her. He could barely recognize her: her eyes were red and swollen, her cheeks drawn and covered with scratches as if she had torn herself with her nails, and her hair hung lank and unkempt about her face.

"My sister," he said, and stopped, for a lump came into his throat.

She began to sob and the salt tears welled up once more. "I have tried to pray, but the Mother will not hear me," she said.

"Be comforted," he said, as soothingly as he could. "Solomon is well. He bade me tell you he loved you and would return. What if he goes to war? My sister knows all men must fight, it is our nature. Would you have him hang back, or show himself less than a man?"

She gripped his arms and he could feel her shaking. "Ah, Sittar," she moaned, "if that were all. It is my guilt, mine is the burden. All, all is upon my head. And if he were to die—"

"What folly is this? Guilt, because my sister brought him to sacrifice to Ashtar? It was I who—"

"You do not understand." She shook her head. "The Edomite—that is my doing. It was I who plotted that he should attack. I have weakened Solomon so that all his people will no longer defend him. Do you hear? I made him vulnerable—I! And I brought Edom in strength to strike at him. Oh, folly! I knew it before the altar of Ashtar, for in the morning the goddess sent me a dream of fire and blood, and when I awoke he was gone."

She dropped her head on his knee, and burst out in a torrent of weeping. Sittar looked down at her with a heart like lead. Gently, he put a hand on her back until she had quieted a little, and he said, "But why? Why should you plot his downfall?"

She replied in a muffled voice, "I pray that the Mother never lets my brother feel the greed of rulers. It was my ambition, my pride that drove me to it. And now I pay for it. What shall I do? Tell me, brother, what shall I do?"

The helplessness of these words from Balkis, she who had always been wiser than he, more self-possessed, secure in her imperiousness, touched him more than his own distress. "Come, take heart," he said. "Solomon is not dead, nor will he die. He is a mighty warrior, as I have cause to know, for did I not first meet him in combat? But I will go to him, and I swear to you I will guard his body with my life."

"Not you, Sittar," she said, clutching at him.

"I must. And you must send me, and all your soldiers with me. Surely, my sister sees that this will help to ease her guilt?"

He helped her rise, and led her to the bed. "Dry your eyes," he said. "Now say to me, 'Go, brother, and the blessing of Shams be upon you.'"

"Go, brother," she repeated, in a tremulous voice. "Ah—I cannot! The blessing of Shams be upon you."

He kissed her cheek and forehead. "Rest, my sister," he said. "I will send Shekiah to you. All will be well, I promise you."

She looked after him as if, indeed, he had the power to fulfill such a promise. He hurried down into the hall, where Shekiah was waiting with a tray of food and wine. "Take that to your mistress," he said. "I must go yet a little while without food. It will do me good, no doubt."

He mounted his horse and went to the barracks of the king's bodyguard, where Arunazel and the Sheban soldiery were quartered. He roused out the captain and gave him orders to be ready to march at the first light of morning. Then he wolfed down bread and meat, drank some thin, sour wine, and went off to the palace.

In the hall, the servants were clustered together, whispering fearfully. The remains of the evening meal were yet on the table, and Ahishar the steward was lighting the wicks of one of the bronze lamps that stood in the corners of the room. Sittar said to him, "Go, find the lady Abishag, and say to her that the son of Merisamis is departing. Ask her if she will come down to me."

The man went off, and soon after Abishag came slowly into the room. She stood silently before Sittar, looking at him with level, somber eyes, her hands clasped behind her.

"Abishag," he said, "I have come to say farewell."

"You are returning to Sheba?" she said, in a toneless voice.

"No. I am going to join Solomon, to fight beside him."

"It is your doing, all this," she said. "I have heard how the men of Israel refused to go with the king."

He bit his lips. "Will you not forgive me?" he said, softly. "If I was thoughtless, I will make amends with my own body. Whatever I did, I did in the hope of settling matters between my sister and my friend. And because of my love for you."

She did not reply. He sighed, and said, "I would change my country for Abishag, turn away from my gods and take hers. Is that not enough? Will you not say that you forgive me?"

Still, she was silent.

"Very well," he said, at last. "If you will have it so . . . I will not cease from loving you."

He went abruptly from the room. She lifted her hand to her lips and bit her knuckle, staring after him, and in a choked voice she said his name. But he could no longer hear her.

He returned to the barracks, where most of his men were already asleep, although a few were at work sharpening their weapons and replacing worn thongs. He wrapped himself in a coarse blanket, lay down on a bench and composed himself, and since he was used to the hunt and to raids, managed to fall asleep.

He was awakened by Arunazel in the gray dawn. "All is in readiness, my lord," said the captain. "We wait only for you. And there is a young man who wishes to speak with you, he who was armor-bearer to the king of Israel."

"Zabud?" Sittar rolled over and sat up, rubbing his eyes. "Where is he?"

"Here, my lord prince." Zabud looked pale and thin, and the coat of mail which he wore hung upon him as if too large for him. From its edge protruded the bandage round his shoulder. "I rode in last night from Jericho, but the king was gone. I pray you, my lord, take me with you."

"But your wound, Zabud—"

"It is healed, my lord, I swear it. I wear this bandage only to keep the mail from rubbing it. And my right hand can still wield a sword."

"Very well. You shall go with me and bear my shield."

They mustered outside the barracks, four hundred and fifty Shebans in helmets and greaves of brass, with leather-covered shields strengthened with plates of iron, each man armed with a sword and dagger and a short bow, for they were accustomed to shooting from horseback. They rode out together through the Hinnom Gate and down into the valley. As they went, men came out of their tents to watch them. Sittar reined in his chariot before a large black tent where stood Ittai the Gibeahite, the sour-faced Gadite Elika the son of Ziba, and a third man, red-bearded and freckled, whose face was disfigured by a scar across his lips and two missing front teeth. His name was Gera the son of Rei, and he was one of the leaders among the men of Benjamin.

"Farewell, Israelites!" Sittar cried recklessly. "I go to stand beside my friend, Solomon, your king for whom you are too cowardly to fight."

Ittai drew his bushy brows together. "Were you not a guest in this land," he growled, "I would prove my cowardice on your skin."

"Brother to the Sheban queen," said Elika the Gadite, "your choice is none of our concern."

"No? What, then, is your concern?" Sittar raised his voice, clenching his hands on the rim of his chariot. He looked beyond the three, to the innumerable faces of warriors who crowded round with curiosity. "Hear me, all of you. What is your concern? I will tell you mine—it is loyalty to one's friends. My gods are not yours. But I do not question where my friend worships, nor whom he loves. Neither did Benaiah the son of Jehoiada, nor Joel the son of Abner, nor the men of Philistia who marched in the king's bodyguard. They are men of their oath! *Hail!* in my land we do not measure a man by his gods but by his manhood. To be a man is to have honor, to be fearless, to draw the sword when one's friend is threatened. And Solomon is more to you than your friend—he is your king! But you—are you men? I think not. Get you to your weaving and spinning, run home to your wives. You are not fit to die with."

He seized the reins again, but suddenly the red-bearded Gera called, "Stay!" His freckles were swallowed in a crimson flush, and he had drawn his sword. Sittar, whose own speech had thrown him into a passion, dropped the reins and leaped from the chariot, in the same motion whipping out his sword.

"Well, here I am," he said, in a fell voice. "Do you not like my words?"

But Gera made no move toward him, only said, "You mistake me, prince. As God lives, I am ashamed that a stranger should show me my duty." And as Sittar stood fixed in surprise, the other turned and shouted, "Where is my armor-bearer? Bring my horse and my shield. Men of my thousand—arm!"

Elika the son of Ziba caught at him. Gera then swung round, took the Gadite by the collar and flung him to the ground. "Are you a man of the hosts of Israel?" he said. "A black day was it for me when I listened to you."

By now, the captains of other thousands had pressed near, and Gera glared round at them. "I will go with the prince of Sheba," he cried, shaking his sword in the air. "Who comes with me? You, Eliam? A hero of the Thirty—will you hide at home? You, Bichri? Jashen? Ikkesh?"

Only an instant did they hesitate. Then, with a roar they took fire from this one spark; one after another they called for their thousands, the men of Benjamin first, then those of Gad, and then the hundreds of Reuben and Gilead. Horns began to sound, men ran to their neighing steeds, weapons flashed in the rising sun and the hillsides seethed like an anthill.

Sittar drove his sword back into the sheath, and with one stride sprang to his chariot. "The king has near a full day's start of us!" he cried. "We must be swifter than the whirlwind. Follow, follow!"

Without waiting longer, he laid the whip across the backs of his team and his chariot plunged forward into the rising dust.

Toward evening, Abishag, muffled in a veil and cloak, came to the house of Balkis, whither she had been conducted by one of the queen's serving-women. She was led up to the bedchamber, where Balkis sat alone beside the window. Abishag made obeisance, and Balkis waved away the maidservant and went to stand beside the Shunammite.

"You are she whom Solomon calls sister," she said, looking into the eyes of Abishag, "and for whose sake he quarreled with his mother and his brother. Do you love him deeply?"

Abishag uttered a sigh. "I am his servant," she replied. "But I cannot hide it from the queen—it is her brother, Sittar, who has taken my heart."

"Sittar?" Balkis stared. "He has told me nothing of this."

"He has loved me for many weeks. And I—I let him go forth without telling him—"

Her voice broke. At that, Balkis clasped her in her arms, and they wept together. After a little, they dried their eyes and sat down together holding hands like two sisters.

Then at Balkis' urging, Abishag told her all, of how Sittar had comforted her in her loneliness and how they had grown intimate, of how she had been set against him, and of their parting. "And when, this morning, I heard that he was gone," she said, "then I knew he was more precious to me than my king, or my own life. He has gone to face death, and I did not even forgive him. Ah," she added, with a woebegone look, "what was there to forgive? He did all for me, and I turned from him."

Balkis said gently, "Do not accuse yourself. The guilt of Abishag is as nothing beside my guilt. And my love also has left me . . ."

She bowed her head. "I caused you to be brought here to teach me how to call upon your God," she said.

Abishag gazed at her in wonder. "I? To teach the queen?"

"Last night," said Balkis, "I went once more to the top of the Mount of Olives, and burned incense and sacrificed two doves to my Goddess. All night I called to her whose servant and queen I am, but there came no response. And I perceived that the safety of Solomon is in the hands of his own God. I must humble myself, even I the queen; I must let your God see my sorrow and my contrition and it may be that he will spare the life of Solomon. For over my love, I fear, the hand of the Goddess has no power."

When she had done, they sat in silence for a while and Abishag said, "I cannot teach the queen. But I will take her before the God of Israel. Cover your face that none may know you, and let us go out as secretly as we may."

Accordingly, the queen veiled herself and wrapped a dark gray cloak about her body, and then she led Abishag out of the garden by a postern door. Through the narrow, dim streets they went close together, and in many houses lamps burned and there came the sound of lamentation and weeping of women who feared for their sons and husbands. They went up the causeway to Moriah, past the unfinished buildings and scaffoldings, up to the gates of the Temple. The gates stood wide and from within came the smell of roasting flesh mingled with the smoke of incense. The priests were at work, sacrificing upon the altar for the soldiers of Israel, and Zadok stood before the Holy of Holies imploring the help of God. At one side, a choir of Levites sang the mighty hymn written by David, their voices pouring forth accompanied by the grave music of harps:

> Blessed be the Lord, my rock,
> Who trains my hands for war,
> My fingers for battle;
> My refuge and fortress,
> My precipice and my deliverer . . .

Abishag and Balkis entered by a side gate which opened into the women's section, separated from the main hall of the Temple by a carved grill of olivewood, gilded and painted. Through the interstices streamed the lights of hundreds of lamps, and they could see the subdued gleam of gold and the innumerable carvings, obscured by the steam of the sacrifices.

Balkis gazed about for something on which to fix her devotion. She said to Abishag, "Where is the image of your God? Is it within, there, behind that curtain?" And she pointed to the Holy of Holies, the doors of which stood open, although the interior was hidden by a thin, embroidered hanging of linen.

"There is no image, neither there nor anywhere," answered the Shunammite. "Our God has no form."

Balkis shook her head. "How, then, shall I address myself to him?"

"Lady," said Abishag, "I do not know. We speak to him in our hearts, for he is everywhere and hears us when we cry to him, for we are his chosen ones."

Balkis sighed. She rested her hands against the carved screen and stared out into the Temple. Her thoughts were full of confusion and she found it difficult to pray, not being able to visualize the deity to whom she spoke. And since she saw no tangible manifestation of his presence, nor any attribute of him, she could not concentrate her desire.

And what was her desire? She did not even know what to pray for. "Spare Solomon's life," she thought. Yes, but was that all? Was there some miraculous answer that should solve the problem of their love? He had not spoken to her of that night when they sacrificed before Ashtar, nor had he told her whether the Goddess had sent him any response; she felt certain that he would have done so had there been anything good to tell. What would the Goddess have said? That which she said to all men who supplicated her: "Give yourself to me utterly, and I will help you." She could not imagine Solomon doing so.

It was, then, hopeless. Must they part? Or would Solomon hammer his head in vain against the wall between them, have her in despite of his people and his God and so bring them all down to ruin? Perhaps his death in battle would be better, far better . . . or let him return to find her gone, and so all things solved.

What was best? She pressed her forehead against the grill, looking into the misty Temple with eyes that ached. And then, strangely, the sense of an ineffable Emptiness crept over her.

There was nothing in the Temple.

All her gods were understandable: they were extensions, as it were, of herself and her people. The Holy Sun, Death, the Mother, the Father, the Lovers, the cold Moon—these were all kings and queens, leaders of tribes, beings both human and divine as she was herself when, clad in the garments of Shams and bearing the horned staff and the pomegranate, she presided over the rituals of the fertile earth. But this God was in no way human: he was within his dwelling and not within it; he existed, but in no way comprehensible by men. There was Nothing in the Temple, a great void full of energy out of which sprang all living things, neither father nor mother, but both in Itself: One, alone, limitless, unknowable.

And feeling this, Balkis shuddered away in fear and bowed herself before the Spirit of creation.

And she thought, submissively, "Thou, God of my beloved, do what seems best in thine own eyes."

Below Hebron, two long ranges of hills curved southward, enclosing between them a fertile, grassy valley more than ten miles long. On the rounded hill crests stood fortress cities guarding the southern road: on the western range, Debir, Anab, Ashan, and En Rimmon, and on the east Zanoah, Jattir, and further south of these, Jeshua. Up the valley had come the host of Edom, besieging one fortress after another and leaving ashes and destruction, and now, at the head of the valley they made camp in the wide, level space below Ashan and prepared once more for the assault.

Solomon looked down on the myriad twinkling campfires, like pale stars reflected in a gray valley. Here, on the heights, the light of day still glowed, and behind him among the low shrubs and stunted trees his small army rested, ate cold food, and warmed themselves as best they might, for he had forbidden them fires.

He said to Benaiah, who crouched beside him, "Mark how heedless they are. They have set out no guards nor any scouts, and they feast and drink as if safe at home."

Benaiah hooked his fingers in his beard. "True, my lord. But would it not have been better for us, as I suggested, had we remained in Debir behind strong walls and defended ourselves? For truly, they are a great host, more than three of them to every one of us."

Solomon smiled at the son of Jehoiada. He knew well what was in Benaiah's mind: that the king had little knowledge of war, and that his chances of coming alive out of the battle were small.

"It is so," he said. "Yet since they are so many, what would we gain? They might hold us pent up with half their force while the other half ravaged on, taking Araba and Ziph, and pushing up to Hebron. Now tell me, in all honesty, if I were not with the army would it be Benaiah's command to skulk in Debir?"

Benaiah was as incapable of deceit as of cowardice. He muttered, "No, my lord. But still—"

"No more 'buts.' I know your thought is of my safety. It is true, I am not skilled in war. Nevertheless, I can see what lies before my eyes: that our only hope rests on surprising them, for when they storm the hills to take Ashan they will not look to find us between them and the city. And if we must retreat, we may take refuge behind the walls."

Benaiah was silent, for this would have been his own plan. They sat on, watching the camp below as the shadows thickened. The sun, sinking toward Philistia, rested upon a rounded knoll to the west, silhouetting the walls of the fortress city, which lay perhaps a mile away. Midway between they had left their chariots and picketed their horses in long lines. To the north, the mountain road fell away in the mists of evening, and all was still except for the low murmur of talk and the occasional clink of armor from the men scattered along the crest and down the western flank of the hill.

The son of David felt no fear. On the contrary, a profound calm was upon him, in which he was able to see, as if for the first time, the loveliness of the world: this mountain world of vapors and pure sky, of folded ravines and long undulating slopes shaggy with thorn bushes and tall dry weeds. Now and again, from far off, came the cry of some night bird, lonely on the heights. A breeze rustled softly among the shrubs, a man laughed near at hand, and from the valley below came a distant murmuring which did not so much break as emphasize the peacefulness of the hilltop.

All this would be shattered on the morrow. Men would suffer and die, perhaps he himself would perish, his fragile flesh pierced and left to rot beneath the sun. Still, he could not summon up fear.

If not now, another time, he thought, twisting a bit of grass around his finger. Solomon will die unfulfilled. What will they say of me—that I was a wise fool, a good king who came to a bad ending? To the dead it matters little what the living say.

He knew that he could not give himself wholly to the goddess, for he could not so easily cut himself off from all that he was, all that had made him king over Israel. Neither could he call upon his God, for he had set aside the covenant between them: he had broken the Law, not once but many times, and all for the sake of a woman. There was no repentance in him, nothing but the thought of Balkis, whom he loved and who loved him. This much at least was theirs, that in their cupped hands they had held the precious jewel which few find; they had looked into each other's eyes and had known each other's hearts. It was enough.

He turned to regard his men, the soldiers who had followed him and might die with him. All at once, touched as he was by the blessed peace, he felt his heart open toward them and a little of what Balkis had given him went out to his companions, a sense of love and kinship, the knowledge that he was not alone. Ah, God of hosts, he thought, I have been selfish, I have been content to be wise for the sake of my pride, but I have never loved them. This, then, was the secret David had possessed, this was why all had been devoted to him—he had given of himself unstintingly, flowing outward toward all men. David had never been content to keep his song within himself, but had sung joyously aloud, never questioning that those who heard would accept and enjoy as he did. Solomon's God was a God of mercy and justice, of peace and law, but David's God was a God of love.

He sank his chin on his hand. The last ray of the sun glistened upon a golden shield, the pommel of a sword, a helmet hung upon a branch. Above, the sky darkened to a color like that of Balkis' eyes. At the king's side, Benaiah stirred and dozed restlessly, and still Solomon sat on, pondering under the tent of night.

With the gray dawn, the braying of battle horns rose out of the valley. Solomon was awakened by his armor-bearer, Eliahba, who brought him a cup of sour wine. The king was stiff and chilled; he had fallen asleep where he sat, and Eliahba had not ventured to do more than throw a cloak over him during the night. The strong wine warmed him a little, and he stood up yawning.

Now his captains came to him, slinging on their swords and rubbing their eyes. He gathered them all together at the hill crest and said, "Behold, the enemy must ascend by the hill road, and when he comes near the top he will be weary of climbing. Yonder is a long, sloping meadow and it is there he will form up his lines for the assault against Ashan. Now, if it seems good to you, we will meet him there while yet he is unready, and hurl him down in confusion. Also, let us fight on foot, for there are many of our men who are unused to fighting on horseback."

"This is a good plan," said Dodi the son of Elhanan, leaning upon his huge shield which two other men might scarce lift. "Only one shortcoming do I see, and that is that we shall be facing into the rising sun."

"As to that, last night a thought came to me," Solomon replied, "which was to place my bodyguard in the center with their golden shields outward. Let them dazzle the Edomite by casting back the sun's rays upon him. As for the rest, let us divide them into two parties, and they may fall upon the enemy from both sides."

"A good word is that," said Benaiah. "As the king has spoken, so let it be. God will deliver the adversary into our hands."

"But hearken," Solomon cautioned. "Bid your men stand fast and silent, that the surprise may be more complete."

The men of Judah, and all the others, then took up their positions, the first two ranks lying down among the bushes along the hilltop, the others crouching behind them. Then they commended themselves into the hands of Yahweh, and began the long wait.

An hour passed, of growing tension and nervousness for those whose first battle this would be; and of last-minute inspection of their equipment, or cat naps, for the veterans. But at length the scouts who had been placed at the extreme edge of the meadow whence they could observe the steep, dusty hill road, ran back and reported that the army of Edom was approaching. To the ears of the waiting men came the clang and jingle of metal, the sound of voices, and the shuffling tramp of many feet and hoofs. And then, over the brow of the meadow, came the dark lines of the enemy surmounted by a glittering aura of spearheads.

Solomon knelt in the center of his forces, looking to left and right. He raised his hand, and his captains readied themselves. More and more soldiers appeared in the meadow, debouching from the road: Egyptians of Aman-Appa's cavalry, clad in dusty linen coifs and kirtles, leading their horses. As they reached the meadow they mounted, and at their head could be seen their captain in a golden helmet, followed by his standard-bearer. He rode here and there shouting commands as his troopers milled in the open. Behind the Egyptians, the lances of another body of men appeared, the horsemen of Chief Timna with Kenaz, the son of Hadad, in the forefront alongside their swarthy leader.

The Egyptians were by now halfway across the meadow, some four hundred of them walking their horses slowly in long lines, holding their javelins idly across the necks of their mounts, and talking and jesting together all unsuspectingly as they went. Chief Timna cursed at his tribesmen to hurry them up the hill and into the comparatively level land.

Solomon motioned to his trumpeter. The man stood up and blew a long, harsh blast, and as he rose so rose the men of the bodyguard, each one advancing his shield.

The sun was now well above the eastern ranges. It shone on the golden shields and flashed in a great dazzle of light full in the faces of the enemy. At the same time, the men on either flank broke from their cover, shouting their war cries. They rushed out like leopards, bounding down the slope to hurl themselves upon the Egyptians.

The cavalrymen had thrown their hands over their eyes at that brilliant light, and fully half were pulled from their horses and slain before they realized they were attacked. In vain, Aman-Appa tried to rally the rest; Dodi the son of Elhanan came up beside him and thrust his javelin through the Egyptian, spitting him from side to side. Aman-Appa seized the haft of the spear with both hands, uttered a shriek, and fell from his horse. The remainder of the cavalry turned and fled. They crashed headlong into Chief Timna's men, with the Judahites at their heels.

The meadow grasses were trampled flat. There was a screaming of horses, clashing of weapons, yelling of frightened men. Chief Timna met with Eleazar the son of Shammah, and they fought together; Eleazar dashed his shield in the chief's face, and pressing in, hewed off his arm with its many silver bracelets. The arm fell to the ground, and the chief stared at it aghast until Eleazar cut him down. The youthful Kenaz, the son of Hadad, fought valiantly surrounded by half a dozen of the enemy until he fell with many wounds.

Almost, it appeared, the battle was ended. The men of Judah pursued the foe down the steep road, and into the rocks on either side. But behind the tribe of Chief Timna were the men of Chief Iram, three thousand of them; hearing the noise of battle above, they had had time to prepare themselves. Iram himself, fat and ungainly, was nevertheless a shrewd warrior, and when the sons of Timna fell back he sent his men into a defile a little way from the road, and led them upward. They encountered almost a thousand men of the half tribe of Manasseh, whom Solomon had placed on his right flank, and among the rocks there was a great slaughter. But the Israelites were outnumbered, and slowly they were forced back until some of the men of Edom came up into the meadow. There they made a stand and were soon joined by others, some of the routed Egyptians and the scattered tribe of Timna. At this, Solomon, who still kept his position with his bodyguard, caused the rams' horns to be blown to recall the men of Judah.

And now the sun rose higher, and yet fiercer grew the battle as its rays beat down mercilessly. Hadad had ridden as close to the head of the road as he could go, and he urged forward the men of the tribe of Pinon. These, fighting their way upward, fresh as they were, pushed back the Judahites on the left. Dodi made a great stand; with one cast of his spear he slew two men, and then he drew his sword, of Philistine iron, and with wide sweeps he mowed a clear space about him while his followers retreated. He was wounded by an arrow in the thigh, but remained on his feet and withdrew when the last of his men was behind him.

Ever more of the Edomites came on, scrambling and stumbling up the rocky slopes or charging into the meadow from the road, and the men of Israel were beset on all sides. Solomon drew his sword and glanced at Joel the son of Abner, who shouted a command. With that, the Cherethites, who had been shooting steadily until their quivers were all but empty, cast down their bows and, with the Pelethites, drew their blades and entered the fight. Behind them, Solomon had placed in reserve the men of Ephraim and these followed the bodyguard.

On his side, Hadad had gone a little apart to a spur of rock from which he could watch the battle. Here he was found by the armor-bearer of his son, who brought him the sword of Kenaz, and the news of his death. Hadad bit his arm in anguish. He snatched up a javelin and slew the unlucky messenger. Crying aloud upon the gods of Edom, he ran headlong into the strife and after him went the soldiers of his guard.

At this time, Adonijah also entered the battle. He had stood aside with Hadad, holding back the two hundred who had come into exile with him from Israel, and when the king of Edom ran down into the meadow, Adonijah shouted, "The Lord God has delivered Solomon into my hands. Victory!" With that, he also charged, followed by his

men. They came upon the left side of the Judahites where Eleazar
the son of Shammah led what was left of his thousand. There commenced a terrible struggle between men of the same blood, and
shortly Adonijah's assault was reinforced by Moabites, allies of
Hadad, who had now reached the field. In that fight Eleazar met
with Adonijah and cursed him; they contended against each other,
and Adonijah beat down the shield of Eleazar, who was his own
kinsman, and stabbed him through the mouth, breaking his teeth
and piercing his brain.

Long and valiantly did the followers of Solomon fight, but they
were slowly driven up the slope to their original positions, and
hemmed in on three sides. Solomon, with a score of his guardsmen
close about him, paused for breath and surveyed the field. His arm
was as weary as if he had been cutting grain for a full day, and his
shoulders ached so that it seemed he could not raise sword or shield
again. God, he thought, tell me what order to give. Shall we stand
or withdraw? Shall we make for the city walls? If we begin once to
retreat, may it not now become a rout?

He stared into the face of Benaiah, who stood close beside him.
Blood from a gash on his forehead had dried in runnels on the commander's cheeks and clotted in his beard. As if replying to Solomon's thought, he gasped, "My lord, let us make one more attempt,
and if we may beat them off for a little space, try if we can get to
the shelter of Ashan."

"Very well," croaked Solomon. He became aware when he spoke
that his throat was parched, and his eyes were burning. He took a
firmer grip on the hilt of his sword, looked to see that young Eliahba
was close by, and gathering his strength rushed again at the enemy.
Benaiah roared out his war cry, and followed hard behind.

From afar, Adonijah saw the tight knot of men, and among them
his brother's gleaming helmet and armor. He drew back and then,
with a shout, hurled himself like one bereft of his wits into the mêlée,
trying to get near Solomon.

This way and that swung the battle, with a hellish noise that
echoed among the mountains. The whole hilltop was as red as sand-
stone, with blood, and covered with the twisted corpses of dead men
or the writhing bodies of the wounded. All this while, Chief Magdiel
of Edom, a wily and shriveled old man, had held his men out of the
fight, watching with narrowed eyes to see how it might go. Now he
saw that the last blow of the Israelites was being struck and it was
clear to him that even though the Edomites recoiled yet they were
still far stronger than the enemy. Accordingly, he raised the standard

of his people and with a shout led them up the road and into battle. After him went the tribes of Teman and Elah, who had been far down the road and had prudently hung back to see what Magdiel would do, for their allegiance to Hadad rested on victories, not defeats.

These thousands, like the surge of the sea, pressed back the men of Israel and Judah, swept around them and cut them off, islanded them among sharp-pointed, flashing waves. Then, grimly, the followers of King Solomon drew together, set themselves shoulder to shoulder, planted themselves like rocks and prepared to die.

Solomon saw before him sun-blackened, sweating faces, glaring white eyeballs, and the flicker of blades: red copper, gray iron, and shining bronze. Blows thundered ceaselessly on his shield, and the golden plates were riven, the ox hide shorn away in strips, and the wood splintered. His helmet was gone, and his wet hair clung to his face. He no longer felt fatigue, but cut and thrust with his notched sword, scarcely concerned to defend himself any longer, borne up by the madness of war, lifted out of himself by berserk fury.

All at once, he was aware of a change in the battle. First, a distant yelling, and a rumbling as of thunder on the mountaintops. Then, suddenly, the men before him melted away: from hundreds they became only scores, and these began to look over their shoulders, to scream incoherently at each other, and at last they broke away and fled. He saw, then, still without comprehension, the horned helmets of Israel, and heard, as the rushing of a deadly wind, many voices exultantly shouting the name of Yahweh, Lord of Battles.

Along the Hebron road, along the mountain crests, had sped the army of Israel led by Sittar. And a little past noon they had come within sound of the battle; without sparing themselves they had whipped up their horses and fallen upon the Edomites. Chief Magdiel's men were the first to fly, and their panic spread quickly. The mounted Shebans in the van, and then the chariots of the Israelites, sped through them, reaped them like grain; within moments all was reversed and the Edomites broken and in frantic retreat.

There were mighty deeds done in that hour. Hadad, desperately gathering soldiers about his standard, met with Arunazel, the commander of the Shebans, and hacked off his head with one blow; he was himself wounded by Sittar, and drawn out of the fight by his armor-bearers, who fled with their lord, clambering down steep ravines to escape. The Ophirite dwarf, Haran, separated from Adonijah whom he had followed, slew two men of Judah; then, seeing that all was lost, tried to surrender. He ran up to the red-bearded Gera, the son of Rei, and held out his sword, saying in his own tongue, "Take me prisoner, Israelite. Let me be a captive." But Gera, without understanding him, dashed aside the sword and felled him. Eliam the son of Ahithophel, who had been shamed by Gera into coming with the host, remembered his great days as one of the Thirty; eighteen men he slew singlehanded, until a stray arrow struck him in the eye and killed him. Joel the son of Abner was twice borne to the ground, and twice his armor-bearer stood over him until he could rise; he met with Chief Iram who was armed with a battle-ax, and catching the haft of the ax as the chief swung it, stabbed him in the belly so that the Edomite's bowels were spilled on the earth. Benaiah, surrounded by a circle of the dead, fell at last; he was not slain by foes but by exhaustion and the heat of the sun.

Sittar at first fought from his chariot; then, when one of his horses was killed, he leaped down and fought on foot. It was thus he encountered Hadad, and after this he turned toward the higher ground where groups of the enemy still held together. Zabud remained close beside the prince, guarding his back but searching ever for Solomon. As the press thinned, and the Edomites went streaming away down the road and clambering down the slopes and cliffs, the armor-bearer at last caught sight of his lord. Without a word to Sittar, he ran at once to join Solomon. Soon afterward, Sittar encountered three men of Chief Iram's tribe. As he fought with two of them, the third got behind him and slashed at his back, and gave him a great wound. Some of his Shebans ran to his assistance and slew his assailants, but Sittar fell.

When the tide of battle had so swiftly turned, Solomon had not realized what was happening. He knew only that the pressure against him was relieved; he lowered his arms and stood swaying, panting for breath. The guardsmen who had been all about him, broke their ranks and began to pursue the enemy. Benaiah and Joel had both been swept away in the fight, and there was none to hold the guards steady about the king. Men ran past on either side of him, or struggled together here and there; chariots dashed through the throng, and riderless horses galloped away in the distance. He looked for his armor-bearer, but the young man was gone.

And as he stared, there came a kind of lull and all the space before him was cleared as if a mist had shredded away before a rainstorm. Not fifty paces away stood his brother, Adonijah, like a graven image of war, his legs planted wide apart, his arms blood-spattered, half the scales shorn from his mail coat, and his long hair flying in the wind. He had no shield, but in one hand he held a dripping sword and in the other a javelin.

A voice said, "Here, my lord! Cast at him."

Turning his head, he saw Zabud. He knew he should be surprised, yet he felt nothing but a dim wonder, like a man dreaming of one long dead. "How came you here?" he asked.

"My lord!" Zabud repeated urgently. "Quickly!"

He put a javelin into Solomon's hand.

The king's fingers closed about the shaft, and without thinking he lifted the spear, feeling the smooth, knotty wood balance on his palm.

Then Adonijah, who had been gazing eagerly about, saw him for whom he also had been searching: the king, his brother and his enemy. And so they regarded each other, motionless, careless of the uproar, a path of silence stretching between them as if Yahweh himself had brought them face to face.

The spear lay heavy in Solomon's hand. I cannot, he said to himself, looking at his brother. All was forgotten save the tall, strong, proud man who had been his friend once, who had comforted him with the offer of toys after the day of the sheep-shearing at Baalhazor, who had saved him from the lion . . .

The lion, he thought. How like they are, the lion and my brother. There was no evil in either of them, they but did as their natures directed.

He saw Adonijah thrust his sword upright into the earth and take his javelin in his right hand. He saw the mirthless grin on his face, and the arm drawn back. The black weapon hurtled toward him. Zabud sprang forward, in front of the king. The armor-bearer tried to hold his shield high, but his left arm was weaker than he thought. The javelin passed over the rim of the shield, entered the base of his neck and stood out a finger's breadth from his left shoulder blade.

As the young man fell, Solomon's mind closed. No longer did he hesitate. In his turn, he cast. Few had ever equaled him in throwing the spear: it went like the destroying lightning from his hand. Almost as Zabud's body touched the ground, Adonijah reeled backward; he sank to his knees fumbling in disbelief at the shaft which protruded from his chest, and then he sank to his side and lay still.

A wordless cry burst from the king. He looked upon Zabud, silent on the trampled grass. Then he went to his brother. Adonijah's eyes were open, his face dusty and set in astonishment. The busy flies were already fastening upon his bloody lips. Solomon knelt beside him and absently brushed away the insects; he touched his brother's cheek and it was still warm, but only from the sun, for the furious heat within was gone.

Then he wept, not only for the dead but for himself, for Zabud, and for all men. He lifted up his face and cried in a terrible voice, "Woe! Woe to Israel that ever had such a king!"

He knelt there incapable of movement, until Joel the son of Abner found him, put an arm about him and helped him to rise. Joel led the king to that same spur of rock where Hadad had stood, and gave him wine mixed with water to drink, and with his own hands poured oil on three great cuts Solomon bore on his body, and bound them up with cloth from his tunic.

While they sat, there came four Sheban soldiers to that place, holding a cloak by the four corners. In it lay Sittar. He had lost much blood but was still alive.

Solomon bent over him, unable to mourn further. Sittar looked at his friend with warm eyes in which still a spark of humor lingered, and said faintly, "Alas, I broke my word . . . I could not remain at home . . ."

Solomon kissed his cheek. "Be still," he said. "The Lord God led you to my rescue."

"As to that, I know not," Sittar whispered. "Yet you have no need to weep over me, for I do not intend to die."

And so jauntily did he speak, in spite of his weakness and pain, that even in his grief Solomon could not forbear to smile.

The Edomites and their allies were utterly dispersed. There had been slain that day nearly four thousand of the men of Israel and Judah, among them many notable warriors, but of the enemy twice that number lay dead on the field. These, the Israelites left to the birds of heaven and the beasts of the field, but all those of Israel who were killed, including the two hundred who had followed Adonijah, were buried in pits on the mountain and over them cairns were raised.

Then they went down to the camp of the Edomites which had been abandoned, where they found much booty and many beasts. They sacrificed to the Lord in thanksgiving, and there they rested and purified themselves before returning to the city of Jerusalem.

# IV THE SACRIFICE

The king's return to his city was greeted with such joy as had not been seen since David brought back the Ark of God out of the hands of the Philistines. Everywhere, the palm branches of triumph waved so that Jerusalem was like a living forest; the air was filled with choruses of acclaim, with the clashing of cymbals, with ecstatic songs. Joining hands, the people danced; they surrounded Solomon's chariot, waving their hands, blowing kisses at him in a kind of delirium, hailing him as the Shield of Israel. It was as if it had needed only this to make him secure in their affections, that like the heroes of the past he should bring back victory over their enemies. "Hallelujah! Praise ye the Lord!" they shouted. "Truly is he the son of David! Behold the Sword of God, the savior, the anointed one beloved of the Lord."

And Solomon rode upon these waves of gladness with an overflowing heart, his eyes dimmed, feeling at one with the nation, sharing with them not only their rescue from the danger of invasion but the knowledge that in his own ways the Lord had once again stretched out his hand over the tribes of Israel to unite them, and thus to save them from a greater danger.

When they had come to the gates, Solomon dismissed his warriors to their tents, and to the leaders and those who had distinguished themselves he gave gifts of great value, swords, brooches, and chains of gold. Then, surrounded by his chieftains, with Joel the son of Abner at his right hand, he went up to the Temple. There, hundreds of cattle, lowing uneasily, had been herded into the outer court, and great heaps of leavened and unleavened bread mixed with oil had been made ready. Zadok, in his vestments, met the king, embraced him, and brought him into the Temple. The thank-offering was made, and when Zadok had dashed the blood to the side of the altar, and placed the fat and the kidneys and liver upon the grate to be burned, the chorus of Levites burst into the psalm of rejoicing, singing with full hearts:

> Therefore I shall praise thee among
>     the nations, O Lord,
> And sing praises to thy name;
> To him who gives great victories to his king,
> And shows kindness to his anointed,
> To David and his seed forever.

Great clouds of yellow smoke rose above the Temple, and the city feasted. Then Solomon went up to his palace, and there at last he removed his helmet and laid aside his gear.

In the hall, his mother Bathsheba met him and fell upon his neck. All her bitterness had been swallowed up by the greater fear for her son's life; she took his face between her palms and looked tearfully upon him, and said in a tremulous voice, "Blessed be the Lord your God, who has brought you home safe and whole."

He embraced her tenderly, and said, "I am happy that my mother has set aside her animosity against me."

She replied, "Let my son forget the words with which I sent him forth. Believe that my folly came only from my love and concern."

Her worn face, webbed with fine wrinkles, was lifted earnestly to him, and he knew a rush of affection that overcame utterly that last memory: he was the child of David and Bathsheba, not of one or the other alone. "I have forgotten," he said. "Let us speak no more of it."

He sat down alone at the head of the table, and his mother brought water for him to wash his hands. Ahishar the steward set food and wine before him, and the king refreshed himself. As he was finishing, Chimham the son of Barzillai came into the hall. Solomon motioned for him to draw near, and the old counselor approached the table and made obeisance.

"May King Solomon live forever," he said, but with an undertone of hesitancy in his manner. "All Israel rejoices that the king has returned in triumph."

Solomon nodded, wiping his mouth with a napkin. It was obvious to him that something weighed on Chimham's mind. "I thank the son of Barzillai," he said. "Now let him say what it is that troubles him."

Chimham cleared his throat. "My lord, it was a great battle, I have heard."

"Yes."

"And it appears that the hand of the Lord was with the king that day."

"The hand of the Lord was upon Sittar the son of Merisamis," said Solomon drily, "for he brought the host of Israel to my aid. Otherwise, I should have been lost."

"Even so. Certainly Yahweh inspired the prince of Sheba." Chimham coughed, thoughtfully. Then he said, "It seems to me—and to Azariah and Shimei as well, for we have spoken of the matter—and the high priest Zadok also—that the will of Yahweh is plain in the matter, and that the meaning of this victory is that Sheba and Israel may be united."

Solomon stared at him. "And the succession?" he said. "You have no fear any longer that a Sheban prince may sit upon the throne?"

"If there is a son by the marriage of Balkis the queen with King Solomon," said Chimham, stroking his beard, "he may be kept in Israel as a hostage and brought up as a member of the priesthood. In the service of God he would relinquish his claim to the throne, or so Zadok believes. If this were agreeable to the queen, we your counselors would approve the union." He raised his eyes to the king's face. "I will not pretend that no problems exist, for my lord Solomon's eyes see deep. Nevertheless, no man can fly in the face of the will of God. A way can always be found . . ."

The king sank his chin on his breast, and remained pensive for a time. Then he rose up, and said, "The love and loyalty of his counselors are jewels in the king's crown. Go to the hall of judgment and wait for me there. Bring together the rest of my council, and I will come to you in a little while."

Chimham bowed and departed and Solomon left the hall also and ascended to his private chamber at the top of the tower. Here, Sittar had been brought and made comfortable, while the king's physician ministered to him. When Solomon entered, he found Sittar lying face-down on the couch with Abishag kneeling beside him, and Balkis seated at his head. The prince was asleep, for the physician had given him wine mingled with poppy seed to keep him quiet and to deaden his discomfort.

Solomon closed the door and leaned back against it for a moment.

He had not seen Balkis since they had sacrificed upon Olivet, and the sight of her made him weak with longing.

"How is it with Sittar?" he said, at last. "What said the physician?"

"That the wound looked worse than it was," Abishag replied. "It is clean and touched no vital part. He will heal if he but lie still long enough, but the prince has been—has been restless—"

She blushed, and Balkis with a wan smile said, "My brother indeed behaved strangely, so that I would have said his wound affected his mind, except that I know this is the way of every man in love."

"I knew that he loved you," Solomon said, gently, looking upon Abishag. "And you—how stands your heart?"

"I love him also," she answered in a whisper. She raised her face, rosy and smiling, her eyes shining, and continued, "My lord, will you permit your maidservant to wed the son of Merisamis?"

He lifted her up, and said affectionately, "My maidservant? No. But I will permit my sister to wed Sittar if it is what she wishes. However, if you go with him to Sheba it may be—"

"Not to Sheba," she broke in. "For he has said that he will remain in our land, and if you will allow him, he will become one of us, and turn to Yahweh and follow his Law."

"Is this true?" He looked at Balkis, who nodded. "Then I am content," he said joyfully, "for nothing will better please me than to have Sittar and his bride always by me."

He kissed Abishag on the brow. Then he said to Balkis, "Come, walk apart with me, for I have much to say to you."

She took his hand, a little shyly, and they went out, leaving Abishag alone with her lover. They climbed the outer stair to the rooftop, and there they stood looking out over the city. The air held a chill, for the season of rains was at hand, and there was dampness on the wind. Fleecy clouds lay upon the horizon, piling one atop the other, and the gardens were full of brown and withered stalks, like ranks of spears.

As with a single thought, they turned to each other suddenly and clasped each other tightly. A long time they stood, warm in this embrace, and then Solomon relinquished her lips and said, "It is as if I had not seen my beloved for many years."

"Why did you not come to me after that night?"

"I could not."

"Could not?"

"I feared to say farewell, lest it be for the last time. And I felt the anger of my God in the news of war—and the coldness of your goddess, as well."

"Yes, I know. And I humbled myself before that anger, and went to your Temple with Abishag, and there I prayed to your God for your life."

He held her yet closer. "You did that?"

"I do not understand the God of Solomon. Yet I will be submissive to his will—and yours."

"Balkis," he said. "Ah—my dove, my precious one. How much you have given me."

Slowly, he released her. He stood a little away from her, and said, "Listen to me, for it is hard to say, and harder still perhaps to understand. Often a man follows his desire and thus works against his own will." He drew a breath, and went on, "In the battle, I slew my brother, Adonijah. The Lord brought us face to face that all might be resolved between us. My armor-bearer, Zabud, stood between us and took in his own breast the javelin that was meant for me. On my head is the death of Zabud, the death of my brother, the deaths of many others who perished—the noble Benaiah, my friend, and young Eliahba, and your own captain, Arunazel."

"No, no," she interrupted. "Not yours, but mine, for it was I who brought Hadad to invade you. That was part of my scheming—"

He shook his head, with a half-smile. "That also I knew," he said. "Sittar told me of it when we were returning to Jerusalem, as I walked beside his litter and spoke to him to keep his mind from his pain. But you were not bound by the Law, as I am; I, not you, broke the commandments of God.

"And how if we had never loved, you and I? If I had held fast to the covenant made between my God and myself? In such a case, you might have seen your plots for empty snares, or, if you had summoned the Edomite in the end, I would have met him with the full power of my people behind me and smitten him with less loss. Zabud might still live, and Benaiah and Adonijah as well."

He swung away abruptly, beating his fist into his palm. "If! If! Who can say what might have been if we had never loved? I have sinned, I have broken the Law, and mine must be the atonement. And for your share of the guilt, you too must pay. And yet, I cannot feel anything but thankfulness for our love—for the little we had that must last me all my life."

She went to him and twined her fingers in his. "Then we must part?" she said, gently. "It seems to me I have long known it. I gave you up when I spoke to your God, placing myself in his hands. Is there no other way, my beloved?"

He sighed. "I cannot wash the blood of my brother lightly from my hands," he said. "And you, Balkis, you know that your goddess cannot dwell in amity beside Yahweh, for my God demands of me my whole allegiance."

He kissed her finger tips, and said, "When I was anointed king I went to the high place upon Gibeon and sacrificed there. That night, I dreamed that the Lord spoke to me, saying, 'Each man must sacrifice what is most dear to him, to receive from me his desire.' That is the fate of kings, that for their people's welfare they must sacrifice themselves. The king himself must lie upon the altar, and must give his flesh to appease the hunger of God. In the face of this, what man knows his own will?

"If we were but simple folk, so that I might say to you, 'Come with me, my sister, my bride, and we will pitch our tent upon the hillside and keep our flocks, and live together in friendship.' How simple, how fair that life would be! But it is not so; I have already said to my God, 'I shall take nothing, I have dedicated myself to you for the sake of your people.'"

His thought ran on beyond the words, and he remembered when he had said them, standing before the Holy of Holies on the day of dedication of his Temple. He had said also, "When the time comes for me to make my sacrifice, lend me the strength to render it willingly and with a brave heart."

Pride, nothing but pride had governed him then! How easy it had been to say those words when nothing had seemed better than to stand before all Israel, spilling from his hands blessings upon those he ruled. But now one desire warred with the other, and it was hard to take up the kingship, harder than he had ever dreamed. His heart's desire? It was not so much that as his destiny, willed to him as the seed of David, to put aside his own ends so that Israel might be great among the nations. All else must give way—even Balkis. And was it not often enough true that a man, doing what he desired not to do, yet might work his own will despite his desire?

And I have this much, he said to himself, that I have known love. And this had awakened him to the love of all men, had given him humanity beyond mere wisdom.

He said, "Like the furnace for gold, like the smelter for silver, the Lord is a tester of hearts. Thus have I been tried, to know if the true metal is in me."

But as he spoke, his voice wavered and a great sob welled up in his throat.

He caught her in his arms, and she clung to him with a pain, greater than any she had ever known, twisting within her. Once more, as her heart broke, she kissed him; then she tore herself free. "Farewell," she said, and went to the stair.

"Wait!" he said. "Turn back. Turn once, that I may look upon you for the last time."

She glanced over her shoulder, one hand resting on the wall, the other flung back a little toward him, her eyes brimming with tears, the sweet, familiar face shadowed with sorrow, no queen but the woman he loved.

She was gone, and he was alone. He would be alone for all the days that remained to him of his life. He rested his hands on the parapet, trying to draw from himself that strength he had prayed for and finding within himself only darkness and emptiness.

He looked out over the roofs of the city, gray now with the clouds that had rolled up over the sun, and whispered, "I sought her whom I love; I sought her but could not find her; I called her, but she did not answer me."

Then he drew himself up, and cried aloud, "Lord, here is your servant, Solomon. I have fulfilled your commandments."

There swept into him, if not strength, peace and resignation. He went forth to place upon his head, once more, the weight of the crown of Israel and Judah.

JAY WILLIAMS was born in Buffalo in 1914, lived for a while in Rochester, and finished high school in New York City. He attended the University of Pennsylvania briefly and returned to New York in 1933.

Then came several years in show business, including four years as assistant press agent for the Group Theatre. In 1941 he entered the Army, got married and began writing a book for children. He served with the 65th Infantry Division from 1943 to 1945 and received the Purple Heart. After his discharge from the Army, he and his wife settled in Redding, Connecticut, where they still live.

Mr. Williams is the author of eight books for young people, two books of non-fiction, including a travel book, *Change of Climate*. He is accounted one of the finest of contemporary historical novelists, a reputation he earned with four books in this field before *Solomon and Sheba: The Good Yeomen, The Rogue from Padua, The Siege* and *The Witches*. He has written poems, stories, and articles which have appeared in many magazines, including *Story, Esquire, The Saturday Evening Post, True* and *The American Scholar*.

The Williams family, which includes a son and a daughter, does a great deal of traveling both in this country and abroad. While at home, Mr. Williams' community activities have included five years as a Cubmaster and participation in many civic organizations. His hobbies range from archery and hiking to ship modeling and photography.